YOU'RE MY I.T.

YOU'RE MY I.T.

C. N. HOLMBERG

PEGASUS

Book Cover Design by Melissa Williams Design
Interior Layout by Kristy S. Gilbert
Editing by Looseleaf Editorial & Production
Proofreading by Jennie Stevens

ISBN 978-1-7370164-1-0

To Kristy, who keeps my head on straight.

Table of Contents

Prologue

BWickers: Hey, Lysander? Sorry—My name is Blaine Wickers. I'm the new hire for the editing department. Aaron said to message you about getting my monitors set up.

LMay: You win.

BWickers: Pardon?

LMay: I can't find any grammar errors in your message.
[GIF of a bunny holding up a sign reading, "Congratulations"]

BWickers: Ha! Thank goodness.

LMay: How many monitors do you have?

BWickers: Two. Well, three, if you include the laptop?
Laptop. That's not a question. Now I'm proofreading everything I type.

LMay: No worries. Be up in a sec.

I dropped my hands from the absolutely horrid ergonomic keyboard IO Masters had left on my desk for me—it was the kind that split in the middle and separated your hands. Also the kind I would risk carpal tunnel to avoid using at all costs. I'd have to ask Lysander if they had a normal keyboard I could use instead, or else I might revert to typing straight from the laptop they'd given me.

I spun a little in my chair, glancing over the short row of cubicles for the technical writers for my new company. I'd finished orientation only twenty minutes ago, but my supervisor was nowhere to be seen. I checked my watch. Five after one. Maybe everyone took late lunch breaks.

My stomach gurgled, reminding me of the cheese and crackers I had in the fridge. Not just any cheese and crackers—I'd packed myself an entire charcuterie board. After rent, my biggest expense went to groceries. If I was going to eat, I was going to enjoy what I was eating. And I *really* enjoyed brie, salami, manchego . . . and just about anything that could fit into the same category as those.

My shiny new job would contribute to more snobbish eating, which was a big plus for me. And I was excited to be in a new environment and meet new people. It was hard to make new friends as a late twenty-something who didn't go to church, especially in a place as religious as Utah. I'd moved to Utah County—what the locals called Happy Valley—six years ago. And the friend thing was . . . complicated.

I opened a few drawers, scoping out my cubicle. It had low walls, which made for a lack of privacy, but I supposed that encouraged productivity, since it was harder to get away with goofing off. *Beggars can't be choosers, Blaine.*

After spinning in my chair a couple times, wondering if I should just take a lunch break, someone finally approached my cubicle. He was relatively tall and tan, maybe of Latino descent. His slacks were too big for him and buckled underneath a drooping stomach that said he also liked to eat. He wore a blazer to hide a subtle Batman T-shirt—IO Masters was business casual, and it was definitely not Friday—that was black with subtle white and gray lines outlining the superhero and his logo. Broad shoulders filled out the blazer well. He had a soft double chin, full lips, and his hair was groomed into a subtle faux hawk.

I stood and held out my hand. "Lysander?"

I seemed to have startled him, despite these short cubicles making my presence clear. "H-Hi," he said and hesitantly shook my hand. He had a firm grip, but he didn't quite meet my eyes.

"Glad you found me." I stepped back to give him space. "I put the cords where they fit, but nothing is popping up on the monitors."

He didn't respond, just set down the bundle of cords he was carrying and turned my laptop around to see for himself. I waited for a confirmation, for a quip, for *anything*, but the guy was all crickets.

He'd seemed pretty friendly on instant messenger.

I picked at a hangnail. "I'm more of a Marvel girl myself."

After unplugging something, he glanced to me. He had . . . really pretty eyes. Brown so dark they were almost black, against bright whites that made them stand out like obsidian on a Florida beach . . . not that we were anywhere near Florida. Or a beach, for that matter. I supposed the closest beach was for the Great Salt Lake, if you liked suntanning in swaths of brine flies.

Lysander looked back at his work.

"Your . . . shirt," I pointed out, starting to feel awkward.

"Oh." He flipped a monitor around, then grabbed a cord from his bundle. "Yeah. I, uh, I like Marvel. Better. But . . . Batman."

I nodded, though I didn't think he saw it. "I get you. Batman is respectable. Especially now that he doesn't wear his underwear on the outside of his pants."

I earned a ghost of a smile, but no response. It was hard to believe this was the same guy who had just been teasing me on the company's instant messenger. This Lysander was . . . well . . . awkward.

Or just really, painfully introverted—admittedly something I wasn't very empathetic with. *Give him the benefit of the doubt.*

And, I reminded myself, this was a tech company. A *deep* tech company. I literally spent hours reviewing things like solid-state storage and MySQL before my interview so I could coherently answer questions, and I *still* didn't get it. But I knew how to use a comma, and my Microsoft Office skills were excellent, so I wasn't too worried.

The monitors flashed on, each showing my laptop screen. Hunching over, Lysander typed onto the keyboard.

"Do you want the chair?" I offered.

"No. Thanks." He did some magic with the keyboard, and suddenly two new desktops populated across my screens.

"Hallelujah!" I clapped. "It's so much easier to edit when you can put the documents side by side. Thanks!"

He didn't give me so much as an *uh-huh*. He picked up his cords and stood there, unsure, for a minute.

"Fantastic Four or X-Men?" I tried.

Another fleeting smile. "X-Men."

"You win." I grinned.

He nodded, stood there for another second, then twisted on his heel and departed. I watched him go. I was pretty sure IT was on the third floor; marketing and the writing team sat on the fourth.

Pulling up my chair, I swept my mouse over the screens, double-checking everything. I hadn't gotten any assignments yet, so my laptop sported only my email and the instant messenger. I pulled up the latter.

BWickers: Thanks again!

Two minutes later, as I was just about to close the laptop and go to lunch, I got a response. He'd sent a GIF of an overdressed prince making an elaborate bow.

Chuckling to myself, I headed to the break room.

There was a pack of salami there singing my name.

Chapter 1

I THINK I FELL in love with Lysander about a year ago.

I saw a lot of him, being the newbie who, ironically, worked at a tech company but knew very little about how computers actually work. He was always awkward in person, but when he was behind a screen, his true colors shined.

> **LMay:** They have a sale on laundry detergent at the Super Target.
>
> **BWickers:** Really?
>
> **LMay:** You should check it out. Should Tide you over for a while.
>
> **BWickers:** You are the absolute worst.

And, because literally everyone in my department, save

Nora, was a passive-aggressive cat-lady, he was one of the few actual friends I had at work. And a much-needed escape from mundane copy edits and asinine document checks with my supervisor, aka the most passivist-aggressivist person who ever passive-aggressed.

Allow me to explain.

Carol Adams has been at IO Masters since she was born (not really, but it feels like it). She wasn't the woman who hired me. No, that woman left two months after I joined the company, and I'm pretty sure Carol was the reason. From my first week I could sense a sort of Cold War thing going on between their cubicles. Carol was technically in the marketing department, but being the most senior writing-oriented person at the company, she sat with the rest of the technical writers. And though she wasn't our boss, somehow *all* of our work had to be approved by her before passing on. I think my original supervisor had been scared of her. Then, one day, my supervisor was gone, and Carol was in her cubicle, and she never explained what happened.

I asked, once. She looked me right in the eyes, then turned around and placed a phone call.

Nora, the other normal person on this floor, has similar complaints about our department—sometimes we eat lunch together or take a break walking around the parking lot to air our grievances, but it has to be *break time*, because if we so much as say a sentence to each other that isn't about SSD devices or semicolon use within earshot of Carol, we'll hear about it in a weird, misdirected, and cold manner during our next morning meeting. Or she'll refuse to check our work and then get on our case about turning it in late.

So Lysander became my outlet. Nora sits too close to Carol for me to send anything in a message to her without risking it being seen over her shoulder.

> **BWickers:** Literally my lunch was moved to the back of the bottom shelf so someone else's lunch box could take my spot. And it's a HUGE lunch box. You could fit two gallons of milk in there.

> **LMay:** I'm guessing this is our favorite someone.

> **BWickers:** The favoritist of them all.

> **LMay:** Unplug something and send in a help request. I'll come up and install a virus.
> [GIF of mad scientist cackling]

I pinched my lips together to keep from laughing. Pulled up the user agreement I was proofing for the *third time* and looked over another half a page before clicking on the instant messenger, which was tucked into the corner of my laptop screen.

> **BWickers:** DONE.

> **LMay:** Wait, really?

> **BWickers:** ;_; Alas, no.

A year ago, I was absolutely stewing over my department. We'd had a writer quit, so our workload was higher than usual, but *everything* was being assigned to Nora. She had two little kids in daycare, and she was pulling in a ton of overtime, while I had literally nothing to do. I talked to Carol about it, but none of the work got shifted. Then, in my six-month employee review, I was written up as "aggressive" and "not a team player."

I had never gotten a bad employee review in my life. And I was pissed as all hell. I vented to Lysander on IM, then to Nora at lunch, then to Lysander on IM, then to Nora on our fifteen-minute parking lot break.

And when I'd gotten back from break, there was a chocolate-chip Frappuccino waiting for me on my desk.

Something about seeing that well-loved dessert next to my laptop, inside a building with absolutely no soul, just broke something in me. Something hopefully good, because the jury is still out on that.

After that, my heart did a little flutter every time my instant messenger flashed. I got excited anytime my software malfunctioned or someone nearby had hardware issues. Because then I would get to see Lysander and his beautifully contrasting eyes, and his secret smile that only a few people ever got to witness.

And he was single. It was my understanding he'd been single since the day I'd met him. I'd not-so-casually asked one of his coworkers in the lunchroom about it a month post-Frappuccino.

"Uh, yeah," he'd said, stirring his microwave risotto. Then he laughed. "Why? You're not *into* Lysander, are you?"

The incredulous way he'd said it made my hackles rise. Like the idea of liking Lysander was laughable.

I'd pointed at his lunch and asked, "Does that have cheese in it?"

And then spent half my lunchbreak listening to him talk about his lactose pills.

> **BWickers:** Doing anything fun this weekend?

> **LMay:** Gaming Friday.

> **BWickers:** Isn't that a Thursday thing?

> **LMay:** Different campaign. I kind of want to GM it, but

> **BWickers:** Remind me what "GM" is.

> **LMay:** Game master. So you're in charge.

> **BWickers:** Right.
> That new Marvel movie is out on Tuesday.

> **LMay:** Oh yeah. It looks good. You going to see it in 3D?

> **BWickers:** 3D is overrated. And overpriced.

> **LMay:** DISAGREE

> **BWickers:** That is . . . I could compromise and see it in 3D . . .

> **LMay:** You should.

That had been my first attempt to get him to ask me out. And there had been so many others. I'd pointed out that the farmer's market was opening up, and I would be happy to show him how it worked since he'd never been there. I'd offered to take him to lunch on his birthday, and invited him to lunch with me and Nora. He'd talk about his tabletop games and I'd say I really wanted to learn (which was true). And he never picked up on it. Ever.

Here's the thing. I'm not afraid of people, or of feelings. But I couldn't, and still can't, bring myself to blatantly ask him out. Not only because it might get weird and I'd lose a friend, but because confessions of amore *never* went well for me.

Never. Ever. Even thinking about saying—or typing—*I really like you and I think we should date* made me nauseous. I wasn't prone to panic attacks, but that brought me pretty close.

I could never tell if Lysander just wasn't interested, or if he was utterly clueless. Sure, he wasn't going to be on the cover of *GQ* anytime soon, but surely he knew when a girl was flirting, didn't he?

> **BWickers:** I'm heading over to the café. Want to come?

> **LMay:** I have to sit here and run a diagnostic on this computer. 57 minutes left.
> [GIF of a cartoon baby crying]

> **BWickers:** Booooo. Can I grab you something, then? What do you want?

LMay: Uh . . . do they have smart carbs?

BWickers: . . .
WTF are smart carbs?

LMay: Like complex carbohydrates . . . my nutrition coach gave me the habit of eating only smart carbs for two weeks.

BWickers: You have a nutrition coach?? Since when?

LMay: Since two weeks ago. It's weird.

BWickers: Huh. Good for you.

LMay: I guess. My dad's been really sick and just got diagnosed with type 2 diabetes. We're a lot alike. And I don't want diabetes.

BWickers: Ah! I'm so sorry. You didn't mention it.

LMay: [GIF of ostrich with head in the sand]

BWickers: You okay?

LMay: Yeah, he'll be fine. Fine enough. But it kind of freaked me out. Especially because he thinks he can just take a pill and be fine but the guy sleeps like 16 hours of the day.

BWickers: Yeesh.

Not wanting to lose a second of my lunch break, I hurried down to the café, which was in the same building as IO Masters. The line was already starting to get long, so I slipped into the queue and checked my personal email on my phone. A calendar notification reminded me I had derby practice tonight—I'd nearly forgotten. My ankles hurt just thinking about it—the three-month break after the end of the season had softened me up.

I googled "smart carbs."

When I got to the head of the line, I ordered myself a BLT with extra lettuce and extra mayonnaise, then grabbed one of the fruit cups in their little refrigerator section. My kitten heels clacked loudly through the foyer as I skipped the elevator for the stairs. Might as well start strength training for the season now.

When I reached the third floor, I took a second to collect myself—adjust the girls, straighten my shirt, smooth my hair, which I always wore down at work to hide the electric blue peekaboo that was my subtle way of protesting the dress code. Then I strode over to Lysander's cubicle wedged in the northeast corner against a window.

I was jealous he got a window.

Sure enough, he was sitting there with a Rubik's Cube, feet up on the desk, waiting for a giant tower computer to run a diagnostic on itself. He fumbled with the cube when he saw me and pulled his legs down.

"Here ya go." I handed him the fruit cup and a fork. "Smart carbs."

"Oh hey. Thanks." He popped the dome lid off and punctured a not-quite-ripe piece of cantaloupe. "This is better than barley."

"You can just eat barley?"

He glanced at me. His dark eyes never got less striking. His thick black hair was a little mussed, like he'd been running a hand back through it. I resisted the urge to touch it.

"Yes?" He shifted. "That's why they grow it."

I had never once seen Lysander not be painfully shy around anyone at work, but he and I had come a long way. Almost to the point of normalcy. He didn't stutter around me anymore, which was a big win in my book.

"I thought they just made it for beer."

He chuckled. "Does that mean beer is a smart carb?"

"Definitely."

He gestured to his very immaculate desk. "You can sit if you want." Then he started. "I mean, you can have this chair—"

"Jeff won't miss his." I grabbed the chair in the next cubicle and dragged it over before Lysander could stand and tried not to smile too much. I was just happy to spend the remainder of my thirty-minute lunch break with him.

I checked my watched. Thirteen minutes until Carol would definitely check up on me.

"How's work?" he asked.

"The worst. I have another employee evaluation coming up." I rolled my eyes and shoved bacon into my mouth.

"You know those are rigged, right?"

I nodded. We were rated on a scale of one to five, five being high. *No one* in the company ever got a five. There had been a lot of complaints about it. I guess our supervisors were told not to praise anyone for their work so they'd be incentivized to work even harder than they already did.

"So dumb," I added.

"I got a five once."

I dramatically gawked at him, which earned me a smile. His teeth were all straight except for one canine, which was turned inward slightly. I liked it. "No way."

He nodded. Glanced over the cubicle wall for witnesses. "I think Aaron got in trouble for it. He changed it to a four the next week."

"This place is a joke."

"It pays well."

"It pays well," I agreed. Lysander could always find the silver lining in anything, though IT didn't seem to have as much of a stick up its butt as other departments.

I watched him eat for a moment—I hated silence in conversations, but they didn't bother Lysander. He struggled to spear a grape. I wondered what he'd do if I rolled my chair over and put my head on his shoulder.

Literally my top fantasy right now was having his arm around me while we watched a movie. Rue, my best friend and housemate, insisted I should have been born in the 1800s.

"Doing anything fun tonight?" *Say no. Then say yes to a movie. At my place. Where one of the couch cushions will conveniently be missing.*

NOTICE ME.

"Just packing." He successfully forked the grape.

Realization sang up my spine. "Is it the twelfth already?" I pulled out my phone to check and sank back into my chair. IO Masters was opening a second office in San Jose, and they were sending a team from Utah to help get it running. Lysander was on that team.

He'd be gone for six months.

"Yep." While some people would love the move to sunny California, especially during Utah's smog-choked and gray February, Lysander had been indifferent about the trip since being asked in December.

"Do you want help packing?" *Say yes.* I'd never seen his apartment, though I knew which complex he lived in.

He snorted. "I don't want you folding my underwear." His skin pinked, and he averted his eyes, like he was embarrassed. He shouldn't have been; I'd said much worse. But pointing it out would only make him draw further into his shell.

"How about a ride to the airport?" I offered.

He chewed and swallowed a piece of honeydew. "I have to leave at five in the morning."

"I can be up at five in the morning." *Ugh. Don't lay it on too thick, Blaine.*

He laughed. "Uh-huh." Shrugged. "Thanks, though. The bus runs by my place so it's easy."

I tried not to look disappointed. "You should watch *Willow* on the plane." I'd been trying to get him to watch that movie for a year. With or without me.

He side-eyed me, a smirk on his lips. "You can't just bring your own movie on a plane."

"You can on a laptop."

"You think I have a laptop with a CD drive?"

I shrugged. Feeling daring, I said, "I'll miss you."

Tossing his empty cup in the trash, he said, "I'll still have messenger."

In the world of dating, instant messenger wasn't even a

base. It was like the dugout where all the unused players sat. But it was something. Without messenger, I never would have gotten to know Lysander. "And I'll still have psychological work trauma to share with you."

He checked on the computer before turning his attention back to me. "You should ask to be transferred."

I did. I wasn't from Utah—I'd grown up in Washington. The Palouse, specifically, on the east side. My mom was still there. After my parents got divorced when I was fourteen, my dad moved to South Dakota and remarried, and my younger sister lived in Virginia with her husband.

Yes, *younger* sister. And yes, I *do* get asked about when I'll get married at family reunions. How did you guess?

Anyway, I love the Palouse, but there aren't a lot of jobs up there outside of retail, so I'd moved here shortly after graduating. California sounded utterly pleasant, especially if it included a small office and Lysander. But—you guessed it—Carol turned down my request and sent someone else. I honestly believe she'd done it because I volunteered. If I'd kept my mouth shut, maybe I'd be sitting next to Lysander on that plane tomorrow.

Six months. My chest hurt.

"You okay?" He leaned forward, looking genuinely concerned.

Smoothing my features, I said, "Oh, yeah. Just heartburn." Checking my watch, I sighed. "Back to work."

"Don't quit," he said. I wasn't sure if it was a motivational quip or, in my fantasyland, short for *Don't quit while I'm away.*

I gave him a thumbs-up and dragged myself upstairs.

The next day, Lysander was gone.

Chapter 2

TWO WEEKS AFTER Lysander took off for San Jose, I chucked my skates onto the yellow-upholstered chair I got at a garage sale and plopped onto my sofa with a groan. My skin was tight with dry sweat, my legs and obliques hurt, and I was developing one hell of a bruise on my hip from an impressive tumble during derby practice. My sequin shorts— yep, that's part of my uniform—were riding up my backside, but I was too exhausted to jerk them down. I didn't need to lift my *Blaine Witch Project* tank top to my nose to know it needed to be washed.

Rue, who was my teammate in addition to my housemate and who occupied the basement of our little rambler, pushed past me, ignoring my whine as she shifted my legs to get to the other side of the couch. Her orange bob was pulled up into a funky ponytail with almost more flyaways than bound hair, and her roller derby name—*Rue the Day*—was bedazzled across her shoulder blades.

She literally cut her hair off the same day she stuck those rhinestones on so people would be able to see them regardless of how she styled her hair.

Rue had joined the derby team first, after learning about it when a friend of hers requested she sing the national anthem at one of their games. I came with her and was so mesmerized by the costuming and football-level violence that I spent the next six months learning how to skate so I could join too. I was a blocker, which was essentially derby's version of a linebacker. Rue, who was quick and light on her feet, was a jammer, aka the one who wiggled through clusters of sweaty women and scored points.

"We are going to kill the Pleasant Graves when season starts." She downed the last of the over-flavored water that she kept in a disposable sports drink bottle that was at least four months old. I'd bought her a nice water bottle for Christmas, and she only used it in the bathroom to rinse her mouth after she brushed her teeth.

I pushed sweaty hair off my forehead. "That's because the Pleasant Graves suck."

Rue shrugged and pulled out her phone. "Want me to order food?"

"Yes, please. Too tired to cook."

She scrolled a moment. "Korean?"

I glared at her. "Why are you saying that like it's a question?"

Her tiny fingers quickly had Korean barbecue ordered and driving to our place.

"To shower or not to shower?" I asked.

"Showering is massively overrated. I actually read an article that it's bad for you."

"Ew."

She grabbed my TV remote and started scrolling through channels—we didn't pay for cable or dish, so it didn't take long to realize there was nothing on. She settled on some gameshow I didn't recognize.

My mind drifted back to work. Lysander had been gone two weeks, but today was the first time he'd appeared on instant messenger. I'd audibly gasped when he messaged me asking if I'd murdered my laptop yet. Which had garnered the attention of Carol, so I'd finished a user manual and turned it in before daring to reply to him.

> **BWickers:** Yes, it's dead. I'm communicating through my mouse.

> **LMay:** Impressive. You should work in IT.

> **BWickers:** Eh. The people down there are snobs.

> **LMay:** [GIF of gasping woman]

> **BWickers:** How is San Jose?

> **LMay:** I wouldn't know because I haven't been outside yet. All the new employees came out of the Bronze Age and don't even know what the internet is.

> **BWickers:** [Laughing emojis]
> If you start walking now you could be back by Easter.

LMay: Tempting. But I'm getting plenty of exercise going up and down the stairs here. Elevator is in constant use for furniture moving and the like.

"Whatcha thinkin', Lincoln?" Rue asked, watching as some poor contestant got red punch dumped on her via a bucket hanging from the ceiling.

I groaned. "Lysander."

"Shocking." Pulling her feet under her, she turned toward me. "And what pointless digital flirting did we accomplish today?"

I grabbed a pillow and covered my face with it.

"Did you ask him how big his hard drive is?"

I laughed. "He probably wouldn't get it."

"Dude is dense."

I lowered the pillow, hugged it, then remembered I was gross and set it aside. "Do you think it'd be weird to send him a care package?"

Her eyebrows skewed. "Isn't that something you send to people in third-world countries?"

"No. It's just a package full of . . . care. Would that be weird?"

"Maybe."

I considered. "What if I sent a care package to the entire office?"

She rolled her eyes. "Then it would be crazy expensive, and what would be the point? 'Oh, the entire staff got cookies from Blaine, therefore I must date her' is not the instant go-to in this scenario."

Now I chucked the pillow at Rue, but my arms were tired and I missed, despite her close proximity.

"You know what, do it." She flung a hand in the air. "Send him a care package full of cookies and nudes and lingerie."

I knew she was joking, but I imagined Lysander opening something like that and wondered what his response would be. If *anyone* was nearby to witness it, he'd probably hate me for the rest of my life. He was very . . . private.

"I wish."

"Then just do it. Or I'll do it for you."

I glowered. "Try it and you'll be in the pleasant graves. And I don't mean the derby team."

She snorted.

I chewed on my thumbnail. "Care package is too obvious. Would a postcard be weird?"

"And we're not being obvious because . . . ?"

Groaning, I covered my face with my hands. "Because it's always weird when I am."

She sobered a little. Rue, of course, knew about one of these instances. It had shattered me pretty well. I'd found Rue shortly afterward, and she'd been my lifeline. The one thing that made staying in Utah worth it.

"I mean," she tried, "that was just the one time. The chances of a repeat are null."

I ripped my hands down. "*Not* one time."

Rue considered a moment. "The girlfriend incident . . ." Her eyes widened. "Oh. The YouTube video."

I shuddered at the memory. At the video I could still pull up if I searched it on YouTube. "First"—I stuck out my thumb—"there was Greg Turney in high school, who I asked to Sadie Hawkins, and then he said, 'Let me get back to you, because I know another girl might ask me.' Another girl! Literally told me to my face that he was holding out for someone better."

Rue cringed. "But that was high school."

"And then *neither of us went to the dance*, Rue. The other girl never asked him and he *never responded to me*. It was so awkward. We didn't really talk to each other after that." And I didn't want that to happen with Lysander. He and Nora were the only people who made IO Masters tolerable.

"Two"—I held up my index finger—"was Ryan."

She groaned.

"Who I basically wrote a speech for to tell him how I felt? Because he was a songwriter and I thought he'd *appreciate it?*"

She slumped into the armrest. "You said it was more Monica though, right?"

"It was all of them, in the end." I pushed on a deep soreness in my chest. Enough time had passed that it didn't hurt too much anymore. It felt like a different lifetime, really. I didn't like digging it up or thinking about it.

Monica. Monica, who had become my best friend after I moved to Utah. Monica, who had unfriended me on social media and *blocked me* after the incident. Most of my friends had. Under her direction or not, I'll never know. I always wondered if they actually hated me for what I did or if there was other vitriol that had spread through the vine. Probably from Monica.

Ugh. During our friendship, I'd been crushing hard on our mutual friend, Ryan Sims, who often came to karaoke or movie nights with a woman I thought was his sister. Because Monica had *told me* she was his sister, because apparently Monica liked Ryan too and didn't know how to use her words when I'd confided in her. Looking back, I could see all the signs. She'd been quiet for a while, then suddenly so supportive. When I decided to confess, Monica was all for it, encouraging me, even assuring me that Ryan liked me too. So I'd pulled him aside at a party and told him how I felt, only to find out his sister was not only his girlfriend, but his *pregnant* girlfriend. Ryan was so awkward, and his girlfriend was pissed, and Monica freaking loved all of it. And our group—the only friends I had within seven hundred miles—just turned on me. I'm sure Monica had spun a few things behind my back to make the situation worse, but even if she hadn't, I was so humiliated I don't know if I could have brought myself to hang out with them again.

Losing my friends had been a hard blow, and on top of it all, my heart had been shredded. I'd really liked Ryan. I'd really believed it would work out for us, that our story would unfold like some romance novel.

Both Ryan and Monica were married now. Fortunately, not to each other.

I'm not sure which hurt more, though. Ryan, or Chad.

Chad—or, rather, his friend Casey—was known now only as "the viral douchebag," and my incident with him qualifies as the most mortifying moment of my entire life.

Chad was Rue's brother's best friend's cousin—I'd met him at a Memorial Day barbecue. He was really funny and charismatic, and we got along *so well*. I was sure he liked me too. Rue was sure he liked me. All the signs were there—text messages, accidental eye contact, flirting. But he never asked me out. So after several months, I got the courage to approach him at a party. I'd pulled him aside to the only quiet place in the house—the guest bathroom. And, having learned my lesson with Ryan, I just spoke truthfully. Told him I really liked him, I thought we had chemistry, yadda yadda yadda . . .

He'd turned me down. Said I was a "nice girl" but he wasn't interested. I was confused. Asked him his reasons. He couldn't really give me one, but at least he'd been honest about it. It sucked hard, but that was that.

Or so I thought.

Because I later discovered Chad's friend Casey had set a camera up in the bathroom—which I'm pretty positive is illegal—because he was about to pull a prank on Chad. The prank happened a little while later, and I guess when Casey went in to edit the video, he saw the entirety of my confession and thought it would be hilarious to upload it to his YouTube page.

He had 120,000 subscribers.

To make things worse, it was a Halloween party, and I'd been dressed as Sailor Moon, which only added to the appearance of me being some kind of obsessed fangirl. Because to up the humor factor, Casey had edited what I'd said to make it sound a) creepy and b) like I'd asked him for his reasons a dozen times. He basically put the question on a loop and made me sound like a total psycho.

I got recognized three different times for that video. Twice online and once at the grocery store. It wasn't hard to pick me out—I'd had a platinum blond pixie with cotton-candy streaks at the time (I'd taken my wig off beforehand, because it was cheap and itchy). After being recognized and reading some of the horrible comments on that video, I'd dyed my hair back to its natural brown and grown it out.

Chad and I never spoke again. I have no idea if he had it out with Casey or simply didn't care.

"But—" Rue began.

"But I am a proponent of being forward. I hate games," I interrupted. "But I'm cursed or something. It's never gone well."

I'd had a smattering of short-term boyfriends, but none of them had ever required a confession. They'd all just asked me out.

Which Lysander had failed to do. I knew that was a red flag and I should move on, but Lysander was *so shy*, more so than any guy I'd ever liked, that some stupid, hopeful part of me latched on to the idea that he might have just been too self-conscious to take me to dinner. So I should take the reins.

Except I just . . . couldn't. Even now, years later, those rejections still stung. The idea of lumping in yet another made me sick. If it happened again, I don't know if I'd recover.

I *really* liked Lysander. Like . . . a lot. I liked his closet nerd. I liked his straight thinking and quiet optimism. I liked his competence and lack of judgment and his humor and his stupid GIFs. I liked his shoulders and his eyes and his hair and his nose and his skin, and it hurt thinking about how much I liked those things.

"I can't now, anyway." I glanced out the window, hoping to see a delivery driver, but the street was empty. "He's all the way in California."

"But that's a good thing, right?" Rue shifted closer to me. "If he says no, you won't have to see him."

"Until he gets back."

"But by then it will have blown over, right?"

I frowned. "I'm not sure it would blow over for me."

Her face fell. But she had a point. Lysander wasn't in my department. I would only see him on occasion.

But still, it felt so impersonal, to admit it to him over instant messenger while he was two states away. I guess I could call him, but that was only minutely better.

"But," I said, counting the days to his return, "he would be getting back pretty close to my birthday."

"I'm listening." Rue pulled her hair tie out, and her locks drooped in a sort of matted-Einstein way.

"I could use it as an excuse to get some friends together, and I'd invite him, and it's my *birthday*, so he wouldn't say no. I'd even make sure it wasn't on one of his game nights."

Rue fake coughed to poorly cover up the word, "Nerd."

"Says the LARPer," I retorted. LARPing—live action role-playing—was Rue's first passion, right before roller derby.

She merely rolled her eyes at me. She had no defense, and she knew it.

I ignored it. "I mean, it would be fun. We could do an escape room or something." My courage started to build, and I leaned forward in anticipation. "I'll butter him up between now and then, and then at the party I'll gauge things, and if they're looking good . . . I'll just do it. At the end of the night, when everyone else is eating cake or something."

After I blew out the candles. Then I'd have a birthday wish on my side. I could use all the karma I could get.

"Attagirl." Rue softly punched my shoulder.

I smiled, and not just because Rue's phone dinged that the delivery driver was arriving with our food. "You think it's a good idea?"

She shrugged. "If you want to wait that long, sure, why not?"

I nodded. I'd been waiting for Lysander for a year already.

I could wait a little longer. It would give me enough time to get over myself, get over my past, and seize what I wanted more than anything else.

○ ● ●

Phase two of my confess-to-Lysander plan was about to begin. It was July, one month before my birthday. Not so far out to make it weird, but not so close that Lysander would have made other plans.

BWickers: I have bad news.

LMay: What happened?

BWickers: It's what's going to happen.

LMay: [GIF of a man with his chin on his hands, patiently waiting]

BWickers: I'm, gulp . . . turning thirty.

LMay: [GIF of cartoon mouse laughing on the floor]

BWickers: Do not mock me, young padawan. I blaze the trail for you and your comrades.

I was two years older than Lysander.

LMay: I am in your debt.

> **BWickers:** And since you are . . . I'm having a little
> celebration where me and some people get locked
> into a room we have to break out of. August 19th.
> Will you be back by then?

I pulled my suddenly clammy hands from the keyboard
and rubbed them together. Got a second message from
a developer asking where the style guide was. I copied
and pasted the folder location and popped back over to Lysander.

> **LMay:** Is your birthday August 19th?

> **BWickers:** It's the 20th, but that's a Sunday and
> everything is closed.

> **LMay:** I actually have other plans . . .

My heart dropped to my diaphragm. Other plans? While
he's in California? A month ahead?
  No, he just didn't want to go. He wasn't interested. *Or
he just doesn't like hanging out with people he doesn't know.*
But how much longer was I going to use that as an excuse?
  He's just not that into you.
  I opened my filing cabinet in hopes I still had those crappy
store-bought cookies in there. I didn't. Vending machine ther-
apy it was.
  When I turned back, he'd messaged me again.

> **LMay:** But I might be able to make it. OK if I bring
> someone?

My heart slowly climbed back between my lungs. He was going to change plans to come. To my birthday party. In a medium-sized social engagement that would probably make him uncomfortable.

This was good. This was very good.

> **BWickers:** Of course! The more the merrier. That way we don't get stuck with some randos if we don't have enough people.

> **LMay:** Awesome. Text me the deets.

Text him. Another good sign. I'd had his phone number for a while now, from when I was stuck creating presentations for a conference and he was going out to some food trucks down the road. I'd given it to him so he could text me what was there. And we texted occasionally, but not like we messaged at work. I was afraid of committing some sort of sacrilege against the sanctity of his number.

Carol *hated* phones, so I slipped into the bathroom to text him the deets. He was technically the first person I'd invited—I was prepared to move everything if needs be. After that, I texted Rue.

> **Me:** It's happening!

> **Rue:** About $*&#ing time.

● ○ ●

It probably looked like I was trying too hard.

I had to be trying too hard, because Carol had complimented my hair. And compliments from her were like ice packs in the Sahara.

I'd seen a couple of developers who had been sent over to San Jose return to work yesterday, which had me rushing to the bathroom to put on lip gloss and pinch my cheeks, just in case.

But Lysander hadn't been on that plane. He'd mentioned coming in today when I'd last spoken to him, which was two days ago. Today, I was fully prepared. I couldn't curl my hair without my peekaboo showing, though I was tempted to risk the write-up anyway. I'd gone with a soft beach wave that required half a can of product to keep it in. I'd thoroughly plucked my eyebrows last night. I had donned all the make-ups, including Rue's forty-five-dollar blush. I'd worn a soft pink blouse and even put on a pencil skirt. I hated skirts. They only let you sit in roughly two positions and contributed greatly to chair-butt.

"Hot date tonight?" Nora's voice cooed into my ear.

I yelped and nearly chucked my mouse into my cubicle wall. By default, I immediately turned toward Carol's desk, but it was empty. Was it lunchtime already?

"Uh, ha, no." I smoothed my hair.

Nora perched on the edge of my desk, resting her hands on her baby bump—this was number three, and her third boy. "Trying to impress *me*? Because it's working."

I laughed. "I just felt like it today."

"And nothing special today?" She thought for a moment. "It's not your birthday."

I felt heat prick my cheeks. "Not until Sunday."

She cursed under her breath. "I need to get you something."

"You don't."

She eyed me. "Nothing to do with the San Jose team returning?"

I turned my attention to my work. I'd never outright told Nora that I fantasized about seducing Lysander and having his babies, but he came up in conversation so often that she'd probably figured it out.

My voice turned pleading. "How about, for my birthday, you stop asking?"

She waved a hand. "Of course, of course. Want to go to the café with me? I heard the bird headed out for barbecue, so we won't spoil our appetites."

I glanced again to Carol's cubicle. "I think I'm going to eat at my desk today."

She glanced at my screen. I wondered if she was looking at my instant messenger. Hiding it would state guilt, so I left it there.

   BWickers: You back yet?

And that was it.

Nora patted my shoulder. "All right." She winked at me and departed.

I retrieved my mouse. Opened a file. Saved it to today's date. Scrolled down. Back up.

Pushed my chair back and headed for the stairs.

I took them down to the third floor, where a couple people in R&D were huddled around a sheet cake, catching up with their newly returned coworker. I passed by them and headed toward IT. A new hire was setting up his computer in a row of empty cubicles. Aaron, the supervisor, was also out to lunch—he had a sticky note on his office door that said

Out to lunch. Only Jeff was there, his bifocals perched on the edge of his nose as he hovered a literal inch away from his screen.

Clicking my tongue, I turned back the way I'd come. Maybe Lysander was coming in for a half day. Maybe he was at the café, though he preferred to eat at his desk or really late in the day, when the break room was empty. Maybe he wouldn't come in today at all. Maybe his flight got delayed, or he ate bad airport food—

I was so absorbed in my thoughts I almost ran into the new hire as he carried a monitor under his arm. I jerked to a halt hard enough to jolt my ankle.

"Oh, sorry," I said, at the same time he said, "I like your hair."

"Thanks." I tucked a lock behind my ear and went around him.

I only got a few steps before he said, "This Saturday, right?"

I froze. That voice.

My heart burst into hyperdrive as I turned around and stared at the new guy. He was relatively tall and wore a soft-looking Henley and straight-legged trousers. His hair was borderline shaggy, and a dark, trim beard hugged his jaw. He had broad shoulders and a broad chest that tapered down to a trim waist. A jaw that wasn't too strong or too soft, and eyes so dark they looked almost—

Almost—

My insides evaporated.

"L-Lysander?" I asked.

He adjusted the monitor under his arm. "Yeah?"

And I just stood there, gaping like he was a circus animal,

completely forgetting myself. Because there was no way this was Lysander. Lysander had *at least* fifty pounds on this guy.

But he had Lysander's voice, and Lysander's eyes, and responded to Lysander's name.

And now he was . . . he was . . .

My brain could only come up with one crude adjective.

Hot.

Chapter 3

I DIDN'T LOOK that different to myself. I saw me in the mirror every morning. I washed my body every day. Fed myself and slept with myself. On my end, the changes had been small.

But they weren't small to anyone else, especially those who hadn't seen me while I was away.

The receptionist hadn't recognized me. My boss hadn't recognized me. And, apparently, Blaine hadn't recognized me either. For some reason, that felt stranger than the rest.

I tried to think of something to say that wouldn't sound off. My brain spun through a few choices. "Sorry if it's weird."

Sorry if it's weird? Good one.

Her mouth worked like she was a Muppet—the metaphor made me smile. Then she blinked and said, "No, not weird! I mean . . . smart carbs?"

"And testosterone." That's what my personal trainer had said. "I mean . . . not like, steroids. Just . . . being male."

Sorry if it's weird. But it was starting to get a little weird.

Because everyone I'd run into had commented on it. Like I wasn't aware I'd been on a "health journey"—which was another phrase from my personal trainer. The term was a little too New Age for me, personally.

I didn't want to make it weird with Blaine.

She shifted weight to one foot and tucked hair behind her ear. "Wow. I mean, that's awesome! Goal achieved, right?"

I nodded. Part of me was glad she didn't tell me I looked good, or point out that I'd lost weight, like I didn't know. Like everyone else had, so far. And yet a small part of me kind of wanted her to.

She let out a long breath. She was wearing a skirt—I didn't think I'd ever seen her wear a skirt. Or heels. She looked, frankly, beautiful. The idea of telling her that turned my skeleton into dust, but there was no harm in thinking it. But Blaine had always been beautiful.

"Right," I confirmed. "Diabetes-free." I set down the monitor—it was getting heavy.

I still hadn't visited my parents. Tonight, I would. My mother would undoubtedly make fun of me while my father pushed that there was nothing to be worried about because he was still *alive*, wasn't he? He liked to push *quality* of life over *quantity* of life, but his idea of quality was eating buckets of sugar and watching movies and maybe dying at the age of sixty.

One thing at a time.

Blaine smiled. "Well. Um. Have you eaten yet?"

She was dazzling when she smiled. Her whole expression smiled, not just her mouth. It lit up the room and made you feel like the most interesting person in the world. Even when

I first met her, she made me feel interesting. But Blaine smiled at everyone, so I'd trained myself not to take it too seriously. Not to look into it, not to let it wiggle into my thoughts, not to have those thoughts, period.

Because I had to face it—before San Jose, no one took me seriously. I excelled at not standing out. In most cases, I didn't mind. I preferred it.

In most cases. Now I had to navigate this newness where people actually approved of the amount of space I took up and strangers swiped right on Hooked.

"I haven't." I put my hands in my front pockets, then pulled them out by habit, because *before*, doing that emphasized my stomach and people always looked at it. I checked myself and put my hands back where they were comfortable. "I brought a lunch, though. Chicken and spinach wedged between two pieces of cardboard."

She chuckled. "Very high in fiber."

I smirked. "The highest."

She grabbed a piece of hair and twisted it around her finger—a few blue locks tangled with it. I'd gotten a glimpse of those before, but I had no idea how much of her hair was blue. Almost matched her eyes. "I brought spam musubi."

I raised my eyebrow. "Come again?"

"It's spam, on rice, with seaweed and everything-bagel seasoning." She lit up. "Wanna see?"

I was honestly curious, and Blaine was always good company. "Yeah, sure."

"Meet at your desk?"

"If they haven't sold it yet."

She rolled her eyes. "Be back."

I watched her stride back to the stairs—Blaine never walked anywhere slowly—and noticed her skirt again. Cleared my throat as my phone rang. The ID just read *Ashley*.

Right. Navigating the newness.

Picking up the monitor and sticking it under one arm— these things weren't as heavy as they used to be—I answered. "Hey. How's it going?"

● ● ○

BLAINE

Lysander. *Lysander.*

Holy hell, Lysander.

I literally hadn't recognized him. And not just because it'd been six months and he was extra tan from the California sun. Not only was his body different, but his *face* was different. Still Lysander, but . . .

I tried to process this as I went upstairs to grab my lunch, pacing myself to buy more time.

He'd really done it. He'd taken charge of his health, and boy did it make a difference. *Testosterone.* No kidding. I'd basically suffocated on it during that entire exchange, and I would have died happy.

Reaching the fourth floor, I made my way to the lunch room, frowning once at my heels. They weren't high, but that didn't qualify them as comfortable.

A smile slipped out. Lunch with Lysander. I finally got to spend time with him again. And I'd play it cool, gauge his interest . . . because I *did* want to tell him how I felt. Whether he came home fifty pounds lighter or fifty pounds heavier, the need to say something was bubbling up like elephant tooth-paste. A little gnat fluttered in my stomach at the thought. It would literally be the best birthday in the existence of birth-days if he reciprocated. If he uttered those beautiful words, *I like you too.* If he kissed me . . .

But I was getting ahead of myself. In fact, I was standing in the middle of the break room, getting a strange look from Carol. Shaking it off, I turned on my kitten heel and marched to the fridge. I didn't want to waste one minute I had with Lysander. Who was *back.*

Who was different.

I'd tried really hard not to comment on it. He was still the same person on the inside, anyway, and while everyone liked to hear they looked good, I knew firsthand that those comments could hurt later. Once, in my early twenties, I'd gotten really sick. Giardia, from a fun river-rafting excursion. I'd lost a *ton* of weight. Like, count-my-ribs ton of weight. And everyone complimented me on it. Asked what diet I was on (parasite), what workouts I was doing (they heavily involved the toilet), etc. And, admittedly, I'd liked the attention. But I got better, and I gained back my weight, and the compliments stopped. I'd never thought I was unattractive or unhealthy before, but after that experience, I felt that way. I yo-yo di-eted for a year trying to slim back down because I craved that attention, and it made me miserable. In truth, joining the roller derby league had helped me get my body confidence back. Made me focus on *fast* and *strong* instead of *thin.*

Cheese helped me fill out my bra better, anyway.

Snatching my lunch bag, I practically jogged to the stair-well. I wanted to hear Lysander's opinion on the newest Marvel movie because I knew he'd read the comics, and I could catch him up on the latest office gossip and then just sit back and suck in all the melodies and harmonies of his voice that I'd been missing all year.

Lysander was back, and thick or thin, I couldn't be happier.

○ ● ●

The day of my birthday party was the longest day in my life. Or it felt that way, in the moment.

I was antsy even before I woke up that morning. All night I'd dreamed about escape rooms, awkward things happening, good things happening. . . . I'd half wake up and roll over to go back to sleep, only to have more weird dreams about Lysander and escape rooms. Sometimes Lysander was his old self, sometimes he was his new self, and sometimes he was Jason Momoa but still technically Lysander.

I showered meticulously that morning. Applied makeup with the care of a surgeon and picked out the most flattering-yet-capable outfit I had. I pep-talked myself getting dressed. I pep-talked myself making breakfast. I pep-talked myself in the mirror. I rehearsed a million things I could say, how I could bring up our relationship, how I could pull him aside without making it weird or convince him to hang out after everyone else had gone.

Because I was going to do it tonight, even if the thought of it threatened cardiac arrest. Even when memories of all my previous confessions drained the blood from my fingers and made my mouth dry. Even when I was tempted to look myself up on YouTube and see if that video was really as bad as I remembered.

I didn't. Too soon.

Rue came upstairs a couple hours before we were to leave for Escape Your Doom. After the escape room, we were all coming back here for cake and maybe some games, depending on how everyone felt. Nothing that would encourage people to stay over. No booze, and if anyone complained, I would claim I was supporting Nora, who was pregnant and couldn't participate.

Nothing to ruin tonight, because I *needed* it to go as planned, or I would lose my nerve.

Everything was ready early, so I took to pacing back and forth in my living room, trying to burn off my anxious energy. It was a thing I did when I was upset or needed to think.

"They're going to notice the tracks in the carpet."

I glanced down, swore, and started walking in switchbacks.

Rue laughed. "I'm kidding."

I knew she was, but I couldn't out-logic my nerves. *Just be yourself.* There was nothing I was better at doing, right?

I gave myself another pep talk as I went back and forth across the carpet, until Rue marched over, grabbed me by the shoulders, and said, "You are hot. You are fun." She paused. "You need earrings."

I grinned and hurried to my room. I had my hair up to show off the blue peekaboo and my triangular undercut, which was currently shaved into the design of a lotus flower. My hair girl got skills. I found a pair of dangling blue earrings shaped like butterfly wings and stuck them in, double-checked myself in the mirror, then strode back to the living room.

"I'm ready," I declared. "Let's go."

● ○ ●

Rue and I were the first ones at Escape Your Doom, but we didn't wait long for the other guests. Emily and Yolanda, both friends from the Salt Lake Sinners, aka our roller derby team, came together. Nora showed up next, her baby belly prominent under a tight shirt. She handed me a gift and excused herself to the bathroom. Ben, one of the league's referees, arrived. His eyes went straight to the little gift bag in my hands.

"Was I supposed to bring something?" he asked.

"Nope. This is from my mom-friend." Because mothers were mothering, and that seemed to put Ben at ease.

He nodded, said, "Happy birthday," and went over to talk to Emily.

Tricia and Caitlyn came next, one right after the other—the first was our neighbor, and the second had been our neighbor in Lehi, but moved to Eagle Mountain about a year ago. Nora returned from the bathroom, and the escape room employee came over with waivers for us to sign.

I turned mine in and glanced at the clock. We were starting in two minutes.

"Is that everyone?" the employee asked as he took the last waiver.

"Um, no!" I stalled. "Sorry, two more people are coming. Is it okay if we—"

Rue put her hand on my shoulder and pointed to the front glass doors just as Lysander opened them. He was wearing a navy button-down shirt and dark jeans, and his hair was styled in that sexy way that was half effort and half unkempt. He glanced up, dark eyes meeting mine, and my stomach flipped. Something about him being here, outside the walls of IO Masters, outside of business casual, for *me*, made nippy little shivers rush up my sides and down my arms. Fragments of a million daydreams rushed through my head, like they were playing roulette at which one might become reality—

And then I saw the friend he'd brought. Tall and pale, in a white tank top that read *SL,UT* on it, cute jean shorts, long blond hair, eyelash extensions, and most definitely female.

And he was holding her hand.

The shivers dissipated. My stomach crash-landed into my gut hard enough to make me flinch.

Lysander hadn't brought a friend.

He'd brought a date.

Chapter 4

I WAS OVERREACTING.

My eyes were getting hot, nausea was churning, and I could feel a flush working its way up to my face.

Rue's hand squeezed my shoulder—

"They're here!" I announced, maybe a little too loud. The broadest smile I could manage stretched out my face as I waved them over and my one semester of junior-high theater class rose up like a phoenix bursting from long-cold ash.

The employee gave them the waiver to sign, and I used those few seconds to shove all the feelings down, down, *down* and paint as much good cheer on my face and body as I could, deliberately not looking at Rue, who would know exactly what was going on in my head right then. The flush diminished, I blinked my eyes clear and dry, and I ignored the brewing nausea and cracking sensation in my chest, like my heart was a tortilla chip and this woman's wedge sandals were slowly stepping on it.

But I couldn't just leave my own birthday party. I had to control this.

I offered her my hand. "Hi! I'm Blaine."

She smiled and shook it. I'd been hoping for a limp-fish handshake, but curse her, the grip was firm. "I'm Ashley. I hope it's okay that I crash."

"Totally, the more the merrier. We only have an hour or the zombies get us." And, though it hurt to look at him and those endless near-black eyes, I turned to Lysander. "Thanks for coming."

He smiled and glanced at the poster that had the apocalypse room—the one we'd be solving. "Looks like fun."

It was supposed to be, but as the employee went over the rules, banned our cell phones, and led us into a dimly lit office that had been purposefully trashed, I couldn't appreciate the ambience, or get into the clues, or focus on the cipher Nora found almost immediately. I tried to laugh at the derby inside jokes and show enthusiasm for each new clue found, but I felt like my insides were stuffed with dryer lint.

It was supposed to be tonight. I'd prepped myself for six months to tell him *tonight*.

And he had a girl on his arm. How the hell did he have a girl on his arm when he'd *just gotten back from California*?

I'd missed my chance. Or maybe I'd never had one in the first place.

Rue noticed. She hesitated to play too. And every time I felt her eyes on me, I forced that smile back on, hunted for clues, or found some other way to participate. I tried to have fun. This was *my* birthday party, after all.

But it was hard.

"Blaine!" Nora called, reaching behind a filing cabinet. "I found something, but the baby won't let me have it!"

Sure enough, her stomach was hard-pressed against the side of the cabinet. Savoring a genuine chuckle, I hurried over to help her retrieve a puzzle of interlocking chains that had a key at its center. I tried to pry them apart, with no luck.

"Here, let me." Lysander took the puzzle from my hands. His fingers brushed mine, and it was like live wires caressed my skin.

The tortilla crunched a little more. I smiled a little harder.

To Lysander's credit, he wasn't hanging off his date. He might have been shy, but he was a team player, quietly taking direction from the more flamboyant persons in the room or patiently working out the code to a lock. So while he stood with me, Nora, and the puzzle, Ashley loomed over Ben and Yolanda trying to decode a message with torn pages from a textbook and a flickering flashlight.

"There's a trick to it," he said, turning the puzzle over. "I did this once, but it was a while ago."

"I've never understood these," I offered, proud that my voice was even.

"Is that one a little bigger?" Nora offered, pointing to one of the links.

"Ah, that's it." Lysander grabbed the link, did some sort of weird twisting thing, and the puzzle opened. He genuflected when he presented the key to me, and I laughed.

"My thanks, good sir." I took it from his palm. "But where does it go?"

"Oh! I think I know!" Nora clapped.

I handed her the key and she rushed to the desk, squatting down to reach a locked cabinet. Lysander smiled at me before checking on Ashley. I glanced at the clock; thirty-four minutes left. We were making pretty good time.

Then Emily pulled a lever and the bookshelf gave way to another room. Everyone rushed in to find new clues. Unsure what to do with myself, I sat down by the abandoned cipher and tried to make sense of the others' notes.

I felt weird. Not just because I was trying very hard not to examine the mess simmering simultaneously in my belly and my brain, but because I was usually the one rushing into the next room, pulling levers, and turning things over. I loved stuff like this. I just wasn't feeling it tonight.

It just kind of . . . sucked. And I tried to make it not suck, but I couldn't just flip a switch and be happy. Believe me, I really wanted to. Believe me, I'd tried before.

So I sat down and half-heartedly worked on the cipher. Rue sat down to work on it with me, but I assured her I was fine, and she went into the next room to help. If I was in my right state of mind, I would have worked faster, but as it was, I had only gotten half the alphabet figured out when someone else sat next to me.

Those vibrant shivers returned when I saw who it was.

"They're ready for that." Lysander gestured to the cipher.

I shook myself. "Oh, sorry. I have all the vowels, if they want to play Wheel of Fortune."

Lysander glanced at my work, left, then came back thirty seconds later. I'd figured out Y and F.

He stretched his legs out on the floor and propped himself on his hands. "They correlate to the shapes?"

"The shapes correlate to these Morse-code things, which correlate to the letters," I demonstrated. Glanced at him. "You okay?"

"Yeah. Ashley's just being kind of a killjoy."

I straightened with stupid mean-girl hope at that. "Oh?"

He shrugged. "This is her first escape room. And she doesn't know anyone."

"You don't know anyone," I pointed out.

"I know you. And Nora. And your roommate."

"Rue?" I guess she'd shown up for lunch a few times in the past. They might have briefly met.

He didn't say anything, so I tried to work on the cipher, but I couldn't focus.

"You suck at escape rooms," he said after a moment.

I laughed. "I usually don't." Cleared my throat. "This is just a hard one."

"May I?"

I handed him the notebook. He figured out a few more letters, which got my mind straightened out, and together we finished it pretty quickly. Forcing myself to my feet, I took the cipher into the next room, where black light highlighted runes along the walls.

"Yes!" Emily rushed over and grabbed the notebook. "It's a *T*, not an *S*!"

They decoded the message, which read *March twentieth*.

"But the attack was March fifteenth," Rue said, "which means he hadn't sent the letter out yet."

"It's in the first room!" Yolanda cried.

We all rushed back—I had the pleasure of finding a vial of blue liquid inside a carved-out book, and floating inside it was a paper with the code to unlock the door and escape.

We made it out with three minutes and twenty-two seconds to spare.

• • ○

Nothing about tonight had gone as planned.

But at least this one moment could still follow the itinerary.

I stood at the head of my little round dining table. Rue dimmed the lights. Two thick candles, a 3 and a 0, stared up at me, their wicks flickering. My friends were singing to me, and the off-key music bolstered my mood. Reminded me of everything I had.

My gaze flicked to Lysander as they sang the last line. He hung out in the back, leaning against the kitchen counter, his lips moving, though his voice didn't carry. Ashley stood next to him, singing the words, though her attention was on her phone.

Birthday wish. I still had my birthday wish. And maybe it was a silly thing to believe in birthday wishes. Maybe it wouldn't work, since my birthday wasn't technically until tomorrow. But when the universe threw you even the smallest of bones, you took it.

So the song ended, I wished, and I blew out the candles.

Then I was applauded like I was five years old, but let's be honest, that's the best part of the tradition.

Rue pulled out ice cream and I cut into the yellow-and-chocolate marbled cake with buttercream frosting. I'd doled out one slice before Nora elbowed me out of the way. "The birthday girl does not serve, she *is* served." Then she cut a piece twice the size of the one I had and handed me the plate.

Rue had made the cake. A box mix doctored with chocolate pudding and cream soda. Sitting on the couch, I took a bite and savored the soft sponge and sugary frosting. Sounds may have happened.

"Do we need to leave you two alone?" Emily laughed.

"Maybe." I gave Rue a thumbs-up.

Nora sat down beside me, letting out a loud sigh. "Are you weird about feet?" she asked.

"Um." I swallowed another bite. "No?"

"Great." She kicked off her shoes and propped her feet on my coffee table, then sighed once more for emphasis.

I laughed.

She set her plate on her round stomach. "Open the gift I got you!"

"Oh!" I'd forgotten about it. Felt my pockets, but Rue was on top of things and grabbed it from the counter. Everyone else was chatting and distributing dessert, so I figured I could open the gift without making it awkward to those who hadn't brought one. I was thirty. Gifts were not required.

Inside the little bag was a transparent computer mouse with a little USB fob. I turned it over in my hands, curious. I wasn't in need of another mouse at home or at work, so I was a little confused. "Thanks."

"I took it out of the packaging to put batteries in it." Nora pointed to its switch. "Turn it on."

I flipped the switch, and the mouse lit up in swirling rainbow colors.

I shrieked. "Wow! This is great!"

"It will piss off Carol real nice too."

I laughed. "No rules against eccentric mice, right?"

"Nope." She grinned. "I checked."

I watched the colors meld and spin a moment longer

before turning the mouse off and side-hugging my coworker. "You're the best. I love it."

○ ● ●

LYSANDER

After everyone else had been served, I cut a small piece of cake for myself. I still had six months left in my nutrition coaching, but never once had the program told me *no desserts*. I hadn't had a treat all week, though by now, sugar didn't really have the same draw on me that it used to. I skipped the ice cream—I was lactose intolerant and hadn't brought any pills with me. The buttercream on the cake wouldn't do much damage. Butter was mostly fat, anyway.

Picking up a second plate, I brought it over to Ashley, who tucked her phone away and smiled as I approached. She had such straight, white teeth. Someone like her never would have swiped right on me this time last year. It was strange. But I'd decided to download Hooked about half-way through my stay in San Jose, though I'd set it to Utah since California was temporary. We'd been talking for about six weeks now, though tonight was the first time we'd met in person. I'd taken her to a Brazilian barbecue place before heading over to Escape Your Doom. Good place for protein.

I wasn't sure if inviting a woman to someone else's birth-day party was considered a faux pas or not, but I tried not to think on it. I had no desire to overanalyze my actions and keep myself awake with a round of anxiety tonight. Ashley had said it was fine, and if I poked at it too much, I'd ruin both our evenings.

Her smile fell as I held out the plate. "Oh, no." She waved it away.

I paused. "Didn't you say you were hungry?" She hadn't had much at the restaurant. A salad, I think.

She pulled her phone back out and opened an app. Took the plate, but not the fork—she looked like she was weighing it in her palm. Then she handed it back to me and typed into her app.

"Yeah, *way* too many calories." She turned the backlit screen to me so I could see an impressive graph that read "sponge cake" at the top. "I'll pass." Then, with a smile, she added, "You shouldn't eat it either or you'll get fat." She playfully poked me in the stomach.

I lurched back on instinct. I hated people touching my stomach . . . though, again, it wasn't the same now. This wasn't my cousin making a Pillsbury Doughboy joke. This was my date, who liked me, and I liked her.

But she said *or you'll get fat* like it was a morbidly funny idea, and I was suddenly grateful I'd taken my IO Masters badge off before picking her up—the one with my first-day photo on it, when I'd been at my heaviest. I wondered what she'd think of me if I ate this cake.

But her phone chimed, and she checked it, so I had a bite. It was pretty good. I wondered if Blaine had made it. Finished it off in about six bites.

Some of her friends—Emily, Yolanda, and then either Ben or . . . was it Paul?—wandered in the kitchen, talking very loudly about something. I took the excuse to cross over to the garbage can and chuck my plate so I wouldn't get stuck behind a host of bodies. As I turned, I spied Blaine coming down the hall. Not knowing when the others would leave, I garnered some courage and swept over to her before she could remingle with the others.

"Hey!" she said, as though I'd just shown up. "Everything okay?" She peered over my shoulder, probably looking for Ashley.

"Yeah." I fumbled with what to say that wouldn't sound stupid. I was comfortable with Blaine, but comfort didn't equal wit. That was one of the reasons I liked instant messaging so much. Gaps between responses were acceptable. And I could see what I was going to say before I sent it. "The cake is good."

"Right? Rue made it."

I nodded. "Um, I should probably leave soon."

Her face fell, and I wondered at it. Wondered if she wanted me to stay, and why, and . . . then my auto-wall came up and shut off the idea without me really thinking about it, just like it had with any viable female since I was a teenager. When you're a two hanging around tens, you just learned not to expect much.

"Oh, okay!" Her usual brightness returned quickly, and I figured I'd imagined the rest. "You probably have more, um, dating to do. I mean, with Ashley. Not like you have another date tonight." She rubbed the back of her neck. "I mean, if you did, I'm not judging you—"

I flicked her shoulder. "I'm just not much of a night owl." Never had been.

She nodded. "Right. And thanks for coming." She knit her fingers together. "I'm really glad you came."

I smiled. "Yeah, me too. It was fun." I reached into my pocket. "I got you something. Sorry I didn't wrap it."

I'd spent a week trying to figure out what Blaine might like after she invited me to this. A coworker had suggested Etsy, a place where crafty people sold their goods. I remembered she was from the Palouse—that's where her mom was, anyway—and I'd typed that into the search bar. After some digging, I'd found a pen made of resin that had a wheat stalk encased in it. Apparently, the Palouse was known for wheat, and writers liked pens . . . I figured it would work.

I handed it to her, weirdly nervous, but my pulse calmed when her eyes lit up. "Oh my gosh." She turned it over in her hands. Turned so the light from the living room would hit it. "This is amazing. I grew up next to a wheat field. Did I tell you that?"

I shrugged. "It's supposed to be from the Palouse."

"Really?" She glanced at me. The lighting made her cheeks look pink. "That's . . . really awesome." Her gaze went back to the pen. "I really like this."

At the same time I said, "It's black ink," she asked, "Can I hug you?"

I started. I didn't hug a lot of people. Just one of those things I'd adopted a long time ago. But I found myself nodding, and Blaine grinned and embraced me, one arm over my shoulder and the other under my arm. It was brief, but I felt it through my whole body, like someone had turned on a hot shower over my head.

She pulled back and danced on her toes. "You're the best."

"Ha." I scratched my head just so I'd have something to do with my hands. Glanced back toward Ashley, who was still typing away on her phone, so I turned back to Blaine. "I didn't know you had an undercut."

It was really cool. Like a tattoo in her hair, emphasized by a giant swath of electric blue. I'd actually never seen Blaine with her hair up before today. Never noticed she had a heart-shaped face and a long neck.

She beamed. "Yeah, it's my way of rebelling against dress code." She laughed. "I used to have this funky pixie cut but, uh"—the smile faltered for just a moment—"then a weird thing on the internet happened and I grew it out. Anyway. I hide that, I hide the peekaboo, I hide the tattoo, and we're all happy in our cubicles."

A smile worked its way onto my lips. "You have a tattoo?"

I'd known Blaine for two years, but it seemed like every time I talked to her, she surprised me.

She twisted her pen in her hands. "Yeah . . . I got it in college. It was not fun."

"You don't like it?" I wondered what sort of image she would ink on herself. And where.

"Oh, no, I like it. But my pain tolerance suuuucks." She swept a loose strand of hair from her face. "The tattoo artist asked me probably a dozen times if I wanted him to stop because I was bawling by the end of it."

I chuckled. "Is it big?"

"It's . . . medium."

"Can I see it?" The moment the question left my mouth, my face flushed hot. "I mean . . . sorry, that's rude—"

"Ha! I don't mind." She glanced back at Ashley. "I mean, it's not risqué, but it might look that way."

A devilish glint lit her blue eyes and she grabbed my elbow. "Here. Real quick." She pulled me to the front entryway and flicked on the light by the door. Then started unbuttoning her blouse.

The hot-shower feeling returned, but this time it lingered. "Uh . . ."

"I have another shirt on," she promised. Sure enough, there was a white shirt underneath the blouse. I didn't get a good look at it because she turned around and dropped her right sleeve. On the back on her shoulder, in elegant cursive, read, *Quoth the raven, nevermore,* and above it was a remarkably drawn raven with a pen in its mouth.

Guess I chose right with the gift.

"That's really cool." I almost touched it, then remembered myself and drew back. Stuck my hands in my pockets for good measure.

"Thanks." She buttoned up, and I relaxed a little. Tried again to think about what to say, but she beat me to the punch. "Do *you* have a tattoo?"

"Uh . . ." *No,* I almost said, because I honestly forgot it was there. I didn't talk to people about it, but it felt like some betrayal of an unspoken pact if I denied it. One of those you-show-me-yours, I'll-show-you-mine things. "Yeah."

She gasped. "Really?"

I scoffed. "That shocking?"

"You just don't seem like a tattoo guy."

"What's a tattoo guy seem like?"

She paused, then flexed her arms in a horseshoe shape and stuck out her chin. "I'm macho and have tattoos," she said in a really stupid voice.

I laughed. "Oh yeah. Those guys."

"Can I see?"

My face heated again, but not so bad this time. Again, that *no* pressed into my mind, because that's what I would normally say. That's what I *should* say, or what I'd think I should say.

But this was Blaine. Blaine had always felt . . . safe.

I glanced down the hallway to ensure there were no witnesses, then quickly unbuckled my pants.

Her hands flew to her mouth. "No."

"Sh," I hushed her and turned around. It was high enough on my cheek that I wouldn't completely moon her, though that was kind of the point.

So I pulled the waist of my jeans down real quick and then hauled them back up, like it never happened. When I looked at her, her mouth was in a wide *O*.

"You have a moon," she enunciated every syllable, "on your butt."

Fully clothed, I quipped, "Where else would I put it?"

She snorted and covered her mouth, and it was like I'd won some sort of prize, getting that sound out of her. I wasn't sure I'd heard her snort before. Not like that.

Her voice pitched high as she tried to speak through muffled laughs. "*You have a moon on your butt!*"

"Shh." I grabbed her shoulders, turned her around, and gently shoved her into the wall, like there was an invisible locker I could hide her in. She kept laughing. After a moment, she managed to get some control and wiped a tear from her eye.

"That's amazing."

I shrugged, but smiled. "I try."

"And we have matching stretch marks."

That made me pause. *Stretch marks*. I hadn't thought about my stretchmarks. A wave of embarrassment spread from my navel . . . then stopped.

"Matching?" I asked.

She shrugged. "I'd show you, but I don't want to make your date jealous." She punched my arm. "Get out of here before you turn into a pumpkin." She walked toward the living room and paused, glancing in Ashley's direction. "And she turns into a zombie."

I checked my watch. Was it 10:30 already? And I still had to get Ashley home. If she was hungry, I could stop by a fast-food place . . . if there was one she liked. I should get going, though admittedly, I kind of wanted to stay.

"Right. I'll rescue her." I waved to Blaine, who waved back. I don't think Ashley realized how much time had passed, because when she looked up, she grinned at me and hurriedly grabbed her stuff, then looped her arm through mine as we walked toward the door.

And I wondered when I'd get used to a woman like her liking *me,* because no one else had looked my way in a long, long time.

Chapter 5

BLAINE

I DIDN'T CONFESS to Lysander that night. After everyone wished me happy birthday and had their social fill, they went home. I showered again, because it was the only thing I could think of to wash the mask off. I put on comfy pajamas and got into bed, then stared at my ceiling for the next hour.

"My boat sailed, Mom," I said on the phone the next morning. On my actual birthday. I hadn't even gotten out of bed yet when she called, and I immediately spilled everything to her. She knew all about Lysander and my grand scheme, and she sounded just as sad as I was when I told her about Ashley.

"It hasn't, honey," she assured me.

I shook my head, though she couldn't see it. "My boat's sailed, and I'm standing on the dock, watching it get smaller and smaller." I'd kept my voice pretty even, but it wavered then.

A three-second pause, then, "Good thing you're a strong swimmer."

I laughed, which relieved some of the pressure building in my chest. "Even so, he'd have to let me board."

"Maybe he will."

"We're forgetting about the date."

"Then let's hope things don't work out!"

I laughed again. Sighed. Thought. "I miss you."

"I miss you too, sweetie."

My mom was like me—we both lived alone without any close family, not since my sister married and moved to the East Coast. Once in a blue moon I looked at jobs at the local universities, though there was never much available, and anything that might pop up would be highly competitive.

Then I realized I hadn't done any job searching since the Frappuccino incident. Lysander's Frappuccino.

Feeling emotional, I told my mom I'd call her back and hung up the phone. Stared at my ceiling some more.

It was funny. I'd actually felt closer to Lysander last night than ever before. I'd even gotten to hug him—I'm shocked I didn't turn into a puddle of porridge right then—and I saw the top of his butt. Half of my giggling had been from that fact alone. *I saw Lysander's butt.*

And it had been so comfortable, so fine, and in another dimension, I would have said, "Hey, I like you," and we would have talked about it with the party noises in the background, and I'd know whether my ticket told me to get on the boat or head to the next harbor.

But I didn't have a ticket. Just me, and the dock, and the sea.

And the stupidest thing was that ridiculous tattoo spoke to me, like it was all the good things about Lysander blatantly written out on his skin, and it might have hurt even more than meeting Ashley had because I saw this thing I wanted so badly and I knew I couldn't have.

So, because it was my birthday, I let myself cry. I buried my head into my pillow and cried for the destruction of a year and a half of loving and six months of planning gone down the drain.

And when I was wrung out and dry, I opened my computer, looked up jobs near the Palouse, and finished off my birthday cake.

●　○　●

LMay: Can you break something?
I am bored out of my mind.
[GIF of cartoon starfish with head exploding]

BWickers: Stay away. Danger zone.

LMay: ?

BWickers: A certain someone is eating a microwave FISH TV dinner up here. Poor Nora just took her laptop to the bathroom because the smell is making her sick.
Take a wild guess who doesn't give two effs.

LMay: I wonder if that's HR worthy.

BWickers: Maybe. I asked her to eat in the break room (which also smells), but she did the *tactic*.

LMay: The thing where she ignores you and makes a phone call?

BWickers: Yep. We're beyond passive-aggressive. That was borderline aggressive.
So yes I might break something. But not in this cubicle . . .

LMay: Your dept sucks

BWickers: I hope she doesn't have access to these messages . . .
Not going to lie, I looked at job listings last week.

LMay: Don't quit.

BWickers: Aw, will you miss me?

LMay: [GIF of man on skyscraper looking out over city]

I sighed and minimized the chat window.
How was I supposed to interpret that?

● ● ○

LYSANDER

"You didn't finish your food!" my mom exclaimed as she reached for my plate. My dad had already finished his and was making himself comfortable in his recliner in front of the TV.

I looked at her incredulously. "*You* made me this plate. This is my second plate."

She clucked her tongue. "Look at you. You need to eat."

I rubbed my face. Both my brothers and I were overweight. Er, had been, I guess, in my case. I didn't know what my BMI was currently, but I was supposed to meet with my nutrition coach tomorrow. But I also heard BMIs were something the insurance companies made up to screw you out of coverage, so who knew.

With a dramatic sigh, my mom took my plate and muttered something in Spanish I didn't bother trying to translate. She'd grown up bilingual, since my grandmother had come here from Mexico. I only spoke a little, and more from what I'd learned in high school than what I'd been taught at home. I could understand most of it, but I think my mother preferred that I didn't. That way she could say whatever she wanted—to herself or on the phone with family—without us overhearing and sticking up for ourselves.

I collected cups and took them over to the sink. I'd driven over after work for dinner since Ashley was going to a bachelorette party tonight. I'd only been back from San Jose ten days, but things were going well. Better than they had in years. My last girlfriend had been in college—a friend who gamed with my roommates and me on the weekend. Half the time I was around her she was totally aloof, and the other half of the time she was really into me. It'd been weird.

So far, Ashley was really into me. And I still felt like I was in the Twilight Zone or something. Like California had shifted time and space and this wasn't the same Utah I'd left.

Supposedly, my body was the only thing that had changed, and yet nearly everyone around me acted like I'd been attacked by a body snatcher.

Except Blaine. She was still the same.

Smiling to myself, I plugged the sink and filled it up with hot water. I managed to get the soap in before my mother slapped me away and said, "Go see your father."

I backed away with my hands up and retreated into the living room. My dad was fully reclined, his bare feet propped up, sporting deep, gnarly cracks in both heels. I grimaced. That had to be painful.

I sat on the couch, nearest I could get to him without standing. A replay from a college football game flashed on-screen. "How've you been feeling lately?"

He glanced over at me and rested a beer can on his belly. "Just fine."

The skepticism was heavy on his face and in his voice. Last time I'd come over—after all the shrieking about my looking different—I'd talked to him about his health, about some things that might help with his symptoms . . . and he'd completely shut me down. He didn't want to hear that sugar was essentially poison and that alcohol literally was. "That's what pills are for," he'd stated, and turned up the volume on the TV.

So I didn't bother trying today. Admittedly, if someone had pointed the same out to me last year, I don't know how seriously I would have taken it either. So I dipped my head to the screen. "Who's playing?"

"BYU and Texas." He shrugged, like he didn't care. But TV was how he spent his free time, so we watched it anyway.

"Computer's acting up," he said after a minute. "Won't print."

"You mean it won't connect to the printer?"

"Or something. Maybe you could look at it before you head out."

"Sure." It probably just needed to download a new driver. I swear my parents' printer was from the nineties, and it was a miracle it still communicated with other appliances at all.

Texas scored. My dad whistled and took a swig of beer.

My phone buzzed. I pulled it out and checked it. Ashley had sent a selfie of herself with her friend, who wore a bride sash across her torso.

I wondered if Ashley had any tattoos.

I responded with a clapping emoji and set the phone down.

My mother walked in, drying her hands on a kitchen towel. "You know the Andersons down the street? Their daughter Mia is visiting this week. The one getting a master's degree at the U." The University of Utah.

It took a second for me to remember Mia, but I nodded. "Okay . . ."

"In *psychology*." She nodded her approval. "I'm going to ask her mother for her number. I want you to call her."

I stiffened. "Her computer broken?" It came out deadpan.

She threw the dish towel at me. "No, ask her out! I want to set you two up. I think you'd like her."

I balled the dishtowel up in my fists. "Why?"

"She's only a few years younger than you, and she's very smart, going places—"

"I mean why didn't you try to set us up before?" Dinner

wasn't settling well in my stomach, and I was pretty sure it wasn't because I'd eaten a lot of asparagus. Tension invaded my muscles so quickly it startled me. Why was I so mad about this?

No, I *knew* why I was so mad about this.

My mother blinked, hesitant. She didn't answer. Because we both knew the reason, and neither of us wanted to say it.

Because, *before*, I hadn't been good enough. And it had nothing to do with my health or my shyness. Just my waistline and my double chin.

Forcing my fingers to relinquish the towel, I set it on the armrest. "I'll go fix your printer," I muttered, and fled down the hallway to their bedroom. Before I was out of earshot, I heard my mother talking quietly to my father, probably trying to figure out how to smooth over the situation.

I got to the small computer desk in their cramped bedroom and plopped down. Hit the power button and waited for operating system to load.

I could have just said I was seeing someone and left it at that. I didn't love conflict or contention. I should have just avoided it. At least with my parents, I could just go home and come back another day and it would be like nothing happened. We all preferred it that way.

But . . . this stuff was starting to irk me. Others' behavior, uplifted tones, smiles where there used to be none. I didn't do this for attention. I just wanted to be healthy. My dad had all sorts of medical issues, including fatty liver disease. Diabetes was just the newest one. The one that, I guess, finally motivated me. And I liked being healthier. I liked that I slept better and had more energy. I liked not being self-conscious of how my clothing fit or being paranoid I'd bend over to fix a tower and get plumber's crack. I liked not being out of breath when I went up a flight of stairs.

But I was starting to miss the ignorance of what my other world was like. Thinking I was always in the shadows because I was an introvert, not because my body wasn't valued by the masses. Because it was really, *really* starting to feel like that.

The urge to sit in front of a movie with a half gallon of ice cream pressed into me. I typed in my parents' password. My phone buzzed.

Eager for a distraction, I slipped it out and checked the screen. Someone I hadn't spoken to since high school had messaged me on Facebook. I had to stare at her name and photo for a few seconds before I remembered who she was. We'd been in auto shop together.

> Hey Lysander! How have you been? Feels like just yesterday we were graduating. I saw you live in Lehi—I'm in Pleasant Grove! Maybe we could catch up sometime?

I reread the message. Why did she care about catching up now, when we didn't even bother talking on social media, aka the most noncommittal means of communication there was?

My stomach sank as I remembered. I switched over to my profile. I'd updated my profile photo this week—Blaine had group texted everyone the pictures from Escape Your Doom after our victory. My profile hadn't been updated in a few years, so I'd popped it up there.

New picture. New *me*.

I had a feeling that was why this woman suddenly messaged me. It was flattering, I guess. Everyone claimed I "looked good," now. My photo must have popped up in her feed.

Her message was friendly, sure. But something about it felt so shallow, so ungenuine, that I deleted it, put my phone on silent, and tossed it on to the bed.

I downloaded a new driver. Printed a test paper. Said goodbye to my parents.

Then I drove to the gym and lifted weights until I couldn't feel anything but pure and utter exhaustion.

Chapter 6

BLAINE

I ZOOMED IN on the photo from Escape Your Doom. Specifically on Lysander, who had shied away to the edge of the frame with his date, not quite touching Ben next to him. I was in the middle—I was the birthday girl, after all. But I wished I'd finagled it so I'd been standing next to him.

I guess this was just a sign.

"You've been on your phone for two hours," Rue complained as she shoved her skates into her bag. The Salt Lake Sinners shared their space with a rugby team, who had reserved it earlier this week, so we were set for a later eight o'clock practice.

I hit the Off button and let the phone drop to the floor. "Why do I always like the ones who don't like me back?"

She rolled her eyes. I deserved that. I'd been moping all week. "You don't always like the ones who don't like you back."

I folded my arms over my face. "I do."

"What about John? And what's-his-face?"

"You mean Spencer?" John was my ex, so I assume what's-his-face was Spencer, whom Rue had never met, only heard of. Groaning, I sat up. I wasn't even dressed yet. "I don't know." Spencer was a college boyfriend who'd become my boyfriend after we "hung out" for nearly a year. We'd dated for three months before he went on a study abroad to England and decided never to come back. John had been drunk—I'm pretty sure—when he asked me on our first date, but that had been my longest relationship, clocking in at just under six months. We'd broken up three years ago. It was pretty mutual. Neither of us was really feeling it anymore. And I was pretty sure he had a thing for his stepsister.

Grabbing my ankles, Rue threw my legs off the couch to make room for herself. I sat up to keep my balance. "Get one of those dating apps. Other fish in the sea."

I *hated* the "other fish in the sea" line. Like that was supposed to make me feel better. All it did was point out what a bad fisherman I was. "It's my fault," I grumbled. "I should have been clearer with him before he left."

Rue pinched my thigh, earning a shriek. "How could you have been clearer without jumping on him?" She sighed. "If it's bothering you that much, just call him. Right now. And tell him."

I cringed. "Not while he has a girlfriend."

"Are we sure she's his girlfriend?"

"I think they're still seeing each other." I tried not to be obvious the one time I'd asked after Ashley on instant messenger. He'd said she was good. Which meant he was still in touch with her.

"Look." Rue pulled out her phone and started scrolling through her contacts. "I know a couple guys. They're cute, they have jobs, and I'm pretty sure they don't live with their mothers. I'll set you up."

I stood and headed to my bedroom—I needed to put on my derby gear anyway. "I hate blind dates."

"Everyone hates blind dates." Rue followed close enough to be my shadow. "But we still do them because sometimes they work."

"Emphasis on *sometimes*." I pulled my shirt off and chucked it at my hamper. Missed.

"Point being"—her thumbs danced as she sent a text—"it will help you move on. You've wasted two years on Lysander. You need to move on."

Two years. That number hurt like an exposed underwire. Had I wasted my efforts? My time, my heart? It didn't *feel* like a waste, but maybe Rue was right.

I still hadn't found that switch that turned the feelings off.

I wish I could jump in the DeLorean from *Back to the Future* and go back to January and tell Lysander everything before he left. To see if I had a chance. To get to him before Ashley or anyone else did. To claim him before he . . . changed.

For a moment, I let myself blame Greg, Ryan, Chad, and all their measly tentacles that had crushed the life out of my dating confidence. If not for them, I would have asked Lysander out the day he left me that Frappuccino. And he would have said yes. Wouldn't he have?

"Oh good," Rue said. "He's free."

I spun around and nearly toppled, since my pants were around my knees. "Who's free?"

"Matthew is free." She gave me a feline smile. "Next Saturday. You guys are going to Olive Garden. How romantic!"

"Rue!" I leapt at her in an attempt to snatch her phone but ended up actually toppling over. I kicked off my slacks. "I don't even know anything about this guy!"

"I'll tell you on the way over." She stowed the phone in her back pocket. "So get dressed, or we'll be late."

○ ● ●

LYSANDER

"You're leaving?"

When Aaron, my boss, had called me into the empty meeting room on the third floor, my mind spun through a variety of reasons why. The first was that I'd done something wrong, broken a piece of equipment, made some critical software malfunction, etc. The second was that it was time for my employee review, but as I silently counted months on the way to the meeting, that hadn't added up either. My last one had been four months ago.

Maybe I was getting a raise? Or sent back to San Jose. I didn't know how I felt about the latter.

But no—Aaron sat me down, took a seat across the faux wood table, and said, "I got a job offer with NewTech and I'm taking it."

I leaned back in my chair. "Huh. I mean . . ." I paused, again trying to think of the right thing to say. I knew I overanalyzed my words and needed to relax, but knowing something and having the ability to *do* that something were two different skill sets. "I'm guessing it's a good opportunity."

He nodded. "It is. And I've let the VP know, and I've also

given him my recommendations. Which is why we wanted to meet with you."

"We?" I jumped when the meeting room door opened again, and sure enough, Kris Kenger, the VP of IO Masters, walked in.

I dropped the pen I'd been holding. Started to stand. Second-guessed my etiquette and hovered above my chair for a second before Mr. Kenger extended his hand. "Lysander, how are you today?"

I straightened and shook his hand, focusing on the action so I wouldn't overthink my awkwardness. "I-I'm great, sir. Thought you w-were still in San Jose."

"Got back yesterday." He patted his briefcase, like it meant something, and took a seat at the head of the table, equidistant from Aaron and me. I lowered myself back into my chair.

"You tell him?" Mr. Kenger asked Aaron.

Tell him what? The words piled in the back of my mouth like they were afraid of my tongue.

Was I getting fired? But my last review had been so positive—

"Just getting to it," Aaron said. With a smile. Smiles were good. He met my eyes. "You've been here what, five years?"

I glanced at the VP. "S-Six." *Stop stuttering.*

Aaron nodded. "You do good work. I've never had a reason to mark you up, and you know our systems better than anyone else. Me aside." He grinned at Mr. Kenger.

The VP nodded. "Essentially, we want you to take over IT."

My heart stopped for half a breath. I sat up straighter. "Wait, what?" No stutter there.

"We'll need a new product manager over IT," Mr. Kenger explained. "Believe me, it's a lot easier to promote within the company than to hire from the outside and go through all the pain of training a new guy who doesn't know the software and doesn't know his team." He tipped his head toward Aaron. "When I asked for his opinion, your name came up immediately."

Not Jeff's? He'd been here longer, but . . . I supposed he wasn't much of a people person. And Artem and Kate had both been here less than two years . . . and that made up the entire IT team in Utah.

I stared at Mr. Kenger, wondering if this was a joke, even though it made no sense that it would be. Carefully, like I drove on a road covered in duck-crossing signs, I asked, "You're promoting me?"

"If you want the position, then yes. I'm promoting you."

"And I'm abandoning you a week from Friday," Aaron added. "I can get you caught up on everything you need to know, but it shouldn't be too steep a curve."

I stared, again, for a minute. I had definitely not expected *this.* I had never really aspired to climb up the company ranks—I'd always been happy keeping my head down and getting my share of the work done.

"You'd need to take a management course through the company," Aaron said, "but it's only a week."

I swallowed. "And . . . and I'd be managing everyone else."

He nodded. "I understand that might put you outside your comfort zone. But it comes with a significant raise."

It would, indeed, put me outside my comfort zone. I

would be attending more meetings, delegating tasks, and generally being more hands-on with the entire department. No more hiding in my cubicle and waiting for five o'clock to arrive.

But a promotion . . . I really liked the idea of that. And the raise. But the responsibility, the people . . . I'd have to lead meetings. Take charge. Assert myself. No more hiding in the back corner by myself, doing my tasks, and slipping home right at five.

I wrung my hands together under the table. "Can I think on it?"

Aaron nodded, like he'd been expecting my answer. Guess he knew me fairly well. "Yes, but . . . can you get back to me no later than Wednesday?"

Forty-eight hours. I'd love more time, but I understood there was a time crunch. I was flattered they wanted me—surprised, and flattered—but . . . could I really do it?

"Yeah, definitely."

Mr. Kenger glanced between Aaron and me and simply said, "Let me know."

◦ ○ ◦

LMay: Hey.

BWickers: Hey. What's up?

LMay: Aaron is leaving the department.

BWickers: Really??? I'm sorry. He's a good boss.

LMay: Yeah, he is.

BWickers: I hope his replacement doesn't suck.

LMay: That is definitely the question of the week.

BWickers: Yeah? Do you know who it is?

LMay: Possibly.
[GIF of boy twiddling thumbs]
They kind of offered it to me.

BWickers: !!!!!!!!!!!
Seriously??
What do you mean "Kind of"??

LMay: Not kind of. They did offer it to me. But I'm waffling a little.
[GIF of syrup pouring over waffles]
. . .

BWickers: Sorry for the delay, the harpy was lurking.
Ly, that's amazing!! You should take it!
$$$$

LMay: Ha ha!
Yeah . . . it's a lot of responsibility.

BWickers: Good thing you're responsible.

LMay: [GIF of man glancing around and pointing to self questioningly.]
Thanks. But I'd be in charge of the team.

BWickers: Team is tiny.

LMay: Team may grow.

BWickers: And? Lysander, you're really good at what you do. That's why you've been offered the job. You know how everything works, so you'll know how to direct people. And you're smart and nice, unlike some supervisors around here . . .

LMay: You must be in a good mood.

BWickers: I AM HONEST.

LMay: Thanks.
[GIF of girl blushing]

BWickers: Obviously, if it's going to make you uncomfortable, don't take it. Do you. But sometimes uncomfortable is a good thing. A growing thing. For what it's worth, I think you'd handle it really well. GO FORTH AND CONQUER, YOUNG PADAWAN.

LMay: [GIF of girl blushing]
Thanks, Blaine.

* * ○

I rested the phone on my shoulder as it rang, drumming clammy fingers on my desk. I should probably go up to Mr. Kenger's office and do this in person, but it was the end of the day and he might not even be there. That, and it was easier when I didn't have to face someone. Or, rather, when I didn't have to worry about how I was presenting myself to someone.

The phone rang several times. I was about to hang up when Mr. Kenger answered, which startled me. I'd expected to be routed through the executive secretary.

"Hello?"

"Mr. Kenger? It's Lysander May." I pulled over the sticky note I'd written my thoughts down on. It sounded silly, but it helped me stay organized when I was nervous. And I was nervous.

"Excellent! I hope you have good news for me."

I smiled. "Yes, sir. I'd like to accept the position."

I heard a *thwack*, like Mr. Kenger had slapped his desk. "Fantastic. I'll get the paperwork in order. In the meantime, I need to catch you up on the next project we're undertaking. We're developing an internal infrastructure so customers can connect directly to our back end. It'll take some effort but ultimately will make everyone's jobs a little easier. Aaron has a presentation to show you, if you can catch him in the office. Otherwise, tomorrow morning."

I nodded, then remembered he couldn't see it. "Great." I crumbled the sticky note. "I'll head over right now."

"Looking forward to working with you."

"Same. Thank you."

I let him hang up first, then set down the phone. Kneaded

the sticky note in my hand. Took a deep breath. The nerves hadn't left. They were uncomfortable. But Blaine was right— sometimes a little discomfort was a good thing.

Surprisingly, I actually felt like I could do this.

○ ● ●

BLAINE

I actually really loved Olive Garden, so when Saturday rolled around, I did myself up, blue hair curled into the brown, smacked on some lip gloss, and drove my actual car to meet my date at the restaurant. I didn't take my motorcycle when I was trying to look nice; helmet plus wind wrecked any and every hairstyle.

Thankfully, my fear of being stood up wafted away when I saw Matt in the foyer. I'd looked him up on Facebook, so I knew what he looked like, and he was true to his pictures. He was really tall, I noted as he stood up to shake my hand.

"Blaine? I'm Matthew."

"Hi! It's really nice to meet you. Rue said nice things." I knew he worked in sales and was a swim coach on the side, and that he had all sisters. That was about it. My mom had shelled out forty bucks to run a background check on him when I'd told her about it, and he was clean, minus a couple parking tickets.

Our table was ready, so the hostess led us that way and tucked us into a booth. It was never-ending pasta month, so the place was pretty packed.

We exchanged some small talk, mostly about our jobs, while we looked over the menu. Matt ordered first when the waitress arrived, and I asked for linguini with clam sauce and a side salad. Point for Matt—he didn't order for me. My last *two* blind dates had.

Yeah, not my first rodeo.

I wondered what Lysander's Olive Garden order was. Did he still eat here? Pretty sure all the carbs on the menu lacked intelligence.

"So," I started after the waitress grabbed our menus and sauntered away, "seen any good movies lately?"

He nodded. "I watched a really interesting documentary on the Enron scandal."

"Oh? I love documentaries. You learn so much from them."

"What are some of your favorites?"

I thought for a moment. "There was a really cool one on the mosasaur I watched last time I was home sick. It was amazing."

His brow quirked. "Mosasaur?"

"Yeah, it was like this underwater crocodile dinosaur. It was massive and an apex predator. It had a moving palate with teeth on it so its prey couldn't get away once it bit down." I tried to demonstrate with my hands.

I earned a little chuckle from him. "That's interesting."

"You should watch it. It's on Netflix. *The Mosasaur*."

He shrugged. "I guess I was one of the few boys on the street growing up that was never really into dinosaurs."

"Really?" I thought everyone was into dinosaurs. I mean, T-rex alone . . . "I mean, *technically* mosasaur isn't a dinosaur—"

The waitress returned with our drinks, cutting off that conversation. I took a sip of my Diet Coke while my date squeezed lemon into his water. Blech.

"So, Matt," I tried again, "outside of documentaries, what do—"

"Matthew," he corrected.

I paused. "Isn't that what I said?"

He smiled patiently. "You said, 'Matt.' I prefer my full name: Matthew."

"Oh." I matched his smile. "Okay."

Though internally I was screaming a little. Who didn't like nicknames? Especially innocent and common nicknames like *Matt* for *Matthew*? Reminded me of an old roommate who I couldn't stand. Her name was Brittany. Brit-AN-ny. If you didn't pronounce all three syllables she got super pissed. It was the weirdest thing ever.

I got over it, though I couldn't remember what I'd be asking. I waited a beat for him to fill in the conversation, but when he didn't, I asked, "If you could have any superpower, what would it be?"

His brow twitched. "I . . . don't know. They're not very realistic."

I took a second to process that one. "Well yeah, they're not *realistic*, but it's fun to think about. For me, it depends on the day. Telekinesis would be amazing, but then some-times I think having the ability to just intimidate anyone on command would be really useful."

"You want to be able to scare people?"

"No *people*, but like, internet trolls." A flash of that stupid YouTube video pulsed through my head, of me and Chad in the bathroom, my heart-spoken words autotuned to the pitch of a whine. I swallowed. "Or really passive-aggressive people at work."

Lysander wanted to fly. That had been one of the first

things he'd asked me after our instant-messenger friendship started. *If you could have any superpower, what would it be?*

Matt—excuse me, *Matthew*—stirred his drink with his straw. The ice cubes clinked against the sides of the glass. "Sure, okay. But really, what's the point? And what are you going to learn about me from knowing what supernatural ability I'd want to have?"

I'm learning a lot about you from your refusal to respond, actually. I tucked that away on my long list of things I wanted to say but didn't say for the sake of tact.

So I changed the subject. "Read anything good lately?"

He thought for a moment. "If you mean books, no. I mostly read news articles. I actually have this app that compiles them from multiple resources so you can compare the media bias. Here, let me show you." He pulled out his phone.

"Oh, great," I took a long draw on my Diet Coke, wondering if I should have ordered something stronger.

It was going to be a long night.

●　○　●

LYSANDER

Ashley sat on the couch in my apartment, her long legs crossed. She pulled a nail file out of her purse and began smoothing out her manicure. She'd come over for a movie; the smell of butter wafted through the apartment as I pulled a bag of popcorn from the microwave and dumped it into a bowl. It was the light stuff, which actually tasted pretty good. We'd already gotten back from dinner at her favorite salad buffet.

Crossing the room, I handed her the popcorn bowl. She smiled and set it aside.

Plopping down on the sofa, she squeezed into me. I put an arm around her shoulders. It was nice, sitting like this. Comfortable. Especially since she wasn't trying to attack my face—she was a little aggressive, when it came to that. I always shook it off; my lack of experience and insecurities weren't her fault.

I scrolled through Netflix on my phone. "How about the new Marvel movie?" I'd already seen it, but I didn't mind watching it again.

"I'm not really into superheroes." She tucked the file away and glanced at my phone, waiting for me to scroll again.

I thought everyone was into superheroes now. But I kept the thought to myself. We passed by some chick flicks, documentaries, and then a title popped up that I recognized.

"Oh, I heard this one was really good." I clicked on the thumbnail that said *Willow*. It was an older fantasy movie Blaine had told me to watch on several occasions. She'd even invited me over to see it, once, but I'd passed. It was a while ago, when I still really liked her and was trying to get over it. Blaine had always been out of my league, and I hadn't wanted to embarrass myself. She was just being nice, anyway.

Not that I didn't like Blaine now, but . . . it just wasn't a *thing*. Twos and tens. Just like no matter how much Ashley crooned about that famous singer, Justin whatever-his-name-was, she would never actually *date* him. That just didn't happen. So I'd shelved it.

That was one of the things about the Hooked app that was so strange to me. Last year, I would have shelved Ashley too.

Ashley squinted to read the fine text, then laughed. "Oh my gosh, is that a real movie? It looks so . . . quaint."

I hit the back button. "So that's a no."

She plucked the remote out of my hands, tossed it to the other side of the couch, and slipped onto my lap. I tensed, afraid of where this was going, of what I would say to avoid things I wasn't ready to do without offending her—

"Let's skip the movie," she crooned. "Let's go to the Rise." The Rise was a club in Salt Lake City. "I want to show you off."

"Uh." My mind spun. "I don't really . . . club." In truth, I'd never been to one. Utah wasn't really known for its clubbing scene, and I'd lived here my entire life. I also couldn't stay awake past midnight to save my life, regardless of how much caffeine I pumped into my body.

That, and clubs were essentially the epitome of everything I hated—loud music, drunkenness, sweaty dancing, and a *lot* of people I didn't know.

And something about the way she'd say *show you off* grated on me. I know she meant it as a compliment. I reminded myself it was a compliment. She just . . . never complimented anything outside my looks.

I really didn't want to go, but I didn't want to disappoint her or start a fight. Story of my life. I scrambled for a valid excuse. "I don't really have anything to wear to a club."

"Just wear this." She tugged on my collar, then undid the first button of my shirt. "It's dark anyway. No one notices what other people are wearing."

I doubted that.

I swallowed. "I already made the popcorn . . . maybe next week?"

She frowned. Flicked my nose with her finger and slid off me, sidling up close on the couch.

I let out a breath. "Do you want something to drink?"

"Do you have bottled water?"

I paused, thinking. "Yeah, I think so." I stood up, grateful to get a second to collect myself. Instead of going to the fridge, I went out to the garage, where half a case of water sat near the front of my car. I grabbed two bottles and made my way back to the couch.

When I got there, Ashley had an open smile on her face, like she was frozen midlaugh. My phone was in her hands. "Oh my gosh, is this *you*?"

A cool, tingling sensation traveled from my chest and up into my skull. Ashley was in my gallery, swiping through my photos. I didn't take a ton of pictures, but I had to check in every month for my nutrition coaching, so I had shirtless bathroom-mirror selfies going all the way back to January.

My mouth went dry, and my stomach burned hot. "Who else would it be?"

She swiped to the next photo. "Oh my gosh, you were *fat*!" She laughed as she swiped to the next one. Clicked on the details. "This wasn't even that long ago! Wow. No wonder you're so soft."

My hand went to my gut. But in truth, her expression hurt worse than her words.

She was laughing at me. Like the me in those photos—the me I'd been my entire life—was a joke. I wasn't even *that* big, was I?

The heat in my stomach burst into flames. Gasoline left by Ashley, by the girl on Facebook, by the random people at IO Masters and at the gym and in my own family just lit until my skin felt like it might melt off.

"I think we're done." It was fire in my mouth, but it came out a trickle of smoke.

"Hm?" She just. Kept. Scrolling.

"We're done," I said, trying to speak louder. Trying to keep my voice even. I didn't really have a temper . . . or I hadn't, before.

She paused. Lowered the phone. "What?"

"Yeah, Ashley, that's me," I said, low and hard. "The only thing that's changed is my pants size. And it's pretty obvious that's the only thing that matters to you."

Her brows drew together. She dropped the phone on the coffee table and stood. "Excuse me? I just thought it was funny. Lighten up."

I didn't bother hiding my scowl. "It's not funny to me." I wiped a hand down my face. "This isn't going to work out."

She snatched her purse. "Obviously."

She pushed past me, scoffing as she did so. Marched to the front door, wrenched it open, and slammed it shut.

Her absence didn't do anything to put out the fire, but I was still glad she was gone.

Chapter 7

Hey hot stuff.

I stared at the first of three new messages I had on Hooked—the app I'd downloaded in San Jose when I decided to attempt dating again. In my experience, the best way to meet women was either at church or at school. I wasn't going to either. I did attend church with my parents on holidays, but I also *hated* talking to strangers face-to-face, so it didn't really matter anyway.

I sighed and deleted the message, elbow propped on my desk, chin pressed to my palm. We got a fifteen-minute break for every four-hour block, so I didn't feel bad about checking my messages. Yet now I wondered if I should have.

If I put my old photos on there—if I uploaded the picture Ashley had found so hilarious—how many messages would be in my inbox?

I got it. The world was a visual place. To pretend I wasn't also a visually minded person would be lying. But that didn't stop it from annoying the hell out of me. And it annoyed the hell out of me because it was more comfortable to be annoyed than to be hurt.

And what if I slipped? I was always worried I'd slip. I'd lived a certain way for almost thirty years. What if I couldn't just flip a switch and change? What if I started dating someone, fell in love with them, and then had one too many funnel cakes and they left as easily as they had come?

I opened the next message.

> Hi! So excited we matched! You're super cute. How are you?

It was a nice message. I *knew* it was a nice message. She was being complimentary. And honestly, this app was set up to be aesthetic before anything else. But . . . I guess I was in a bad mood. I didn't delete it, but I'd wait until later to respond. When I wasn't feeling so . . . sensitive.

I clicked on the third message and nearly dropped my phone. Cursing, I fumbled for the delete button.

Someone had sent me a nude, and I didn't even know who she was.

The audacity of it aside, I was at work. What if someone walked by and saw that on my screen?

I heaved a sigh of relief when the photo vanished, then glanced over my shoulder just to be safe. Alone. I was still tucked into my cubicle—I was moving into Aaron's office on Friday, after he said his final goodbyes. *An office.* I was moving up in the world. Professionally, at least.

I glanced at my phone. The screen had timed out. I really did want to advance there too. The dating stuff, that was. I wanted to meet someone, eventually get married, have a family . . . I mean, didn't everyone want something like that? Stuff like Hooked was a necessary evil to get past the first step. I just didn't know how many Ashleys I'd have to go through to get to the Blaines.

I paused. Looked up, like she might be hovering over my cubicle wall, smiling at me.

The way she smiled at everyone.

Get over yourself. Spinning in my chair, I chucked my phone in the trash can. I'd dig it out before I went home.

Opening my email, I saw a message from Aaron with the VP cc'd. More details about the infrastructure project. I had my work cut out for me.

My instant messenger flashed.

> **BWickers:** I'm going to assume you don't want the cake in the break room. Someone had a birthday and someone else really overcompensated.

Smiling, I typed back.

> **LMay:** I'm good. Thanks though.

And got back to work.

● ● ○

BLAINE

"Huh."

I rolled past Rue, half-empty water bottle in hand, and collapsed into the folding metal chair beside her. We were at the training center, which smelled like sweat and varnish and had evening sun pouring through the west-facing windows pressed up against the high ceiling. I'd just finished defensive drills on the floor. My legs were trembling with the effort—blocking a jammer in sneakers would be one thing, but on wheels? Way more difficult. Now the traveling team was on the floor, giving me a second to breathe and nurse the new bruises forming on my body. The first on my ribs where Yolanda had accidentally elbowed me, and the one blooming on my backside from a hard fall. Unfortunately, no matter how practiced one was with derby, bruises were inevitable.

"Huh what?" I asked, unbuckling and pulling off my helmet. I sighed as air swept over my sweaty scalp.

She turned her phone screen to me. "Isn't this Lysander?"

Just the sound of his name made my ears ring. I grabbed the phone and took a better look. Sure enough, it was—an awkward bathroom selfie of him, a third of his face hidden by the phone he was holding. I swiped over to see a familiar zoomed-in shot of him—it was the photo from the escape room.

"Is this Hooked?" I asked as Rue pried the phone from my clammy fingers.

"Yeah." She swiped up to view his profile, and I scooted closed to her to see better. His profile was pretty sparse. 5'11", weight not listed, twenty-eight years old. He'd turned twenty-eight while in California. I'd sent him an e-gift card to a local restaurant.

Rue stole my water bottle and took a swig. "He must have broken up with that blond chick."

My pulse thudded in my neck and chest, and not because

I'd been squatting in skates around the track for the last thirty minutes. "You think?"

"Why else would his profile be switched on?" She swiped left.

"Wait!"

She eyed me. "It searches everyone in a selected radius. Mine is set to twenty miles. So download the app."

I gagged. I hated dating apps. I hated the drama and the hookups and the judgment—people rating each other based on a picture that half the time was a catfishing scheme. It felt so shallow to me.

I licked my lips, tasting salt. But if Lysander was on Hooked, that meant he was single, right?

Maybe I didn't have to be direct. Maybe I could make this easy on myself. Literally slide into his DMs.

Wiping my hands on my reversible sequin shorts, I grabbed my backpack and pulled out my phone. Searched "Hooked" in the app store. Hovered over the icon for a few seconds before giving in and downloading it.

The screen popped up and I groaned.

"What?" Rue asked.

"I have to make a profile."

"No der, you have to make a profile. Just take your photos from Facebook."

Chewing on my lip, I scrolled through my gallery for a picture. You could upload five, but I only needed one. One where I was easily recognizable.

I picked one from my trip to the Palouse last Christmas. I was in my mom's kitchen holding up an unbaked pie that had four swords made from extra crust on top of it, the points all facing in. My hair was pulled over my shoulders, showing off the blue, and my boobs looked good.

I uploaded it. Then, for extra measure, I uploaded the escape room picture as my number two. Put in my basic stats and skipped the interests and about me section. That was optional.

See? Shallow.

I put in my date preferences, selected twenty miles, and I was in.

And began swiping left like a madwoman.

I whistled as photo after photo passed by. There were this many single people in the county? Some of them were cute . . . I considered slowing down and hedging my bets.

But no, I knew exactly who I wanted. There were lots of fish in the sea, yes, but I very specifically wanted bluefin tuna.

It took forever. After ten minutes of thumb aerobics, Rue got up and put a cloth cap with a star on it over her helmet—marking her as a jammer, the one who scored points. She skated out to the track, leaving me swiping.

After another five minutes, Lysander's picture popped up. I shrieked and dropped my phone because I'd nearly swiped left on him. Then where would I be?

Picking up my phone, I stared at his picture. Swiped up to see his stats. Noticed another little up arrow, and swiped up again.

I'd been wrong—his profile wasn't sparse. He'd filled out everything.

Likes: fantasy, science fiction, reading, video games, movies, Marvel, space, alternative music, rock, computers, magic, board games, tabletop games. Dislikes: ramen noodles.

I smiled at that.

I work in the tech industry, so yes, I can probably fix your computer. Maybe your phone. Puns are the lowest form of humor. +10 points if you have a dog.

"I need to get a dog," I murmured to myself, swiping back up to his photo. My thumb hovered over it.

If I remembered right, the way Hooked worked was you swiped right on the people you were interested in. If they also swiped right on you, you matched and could then instant message one another. If they didn't swipe right on you, they never found out you swiped right on them. So it was shallow, yes, but also noncommittal. Rue had complained about Hooked ghosting on multiple occasions, but only with people she matched with, not people who passed her by.

So the worst thing that could happen was that he saw my profile, swiped *left*, and never knew I was pining away for him on the other end of a satellite signal. Best-case scenario . . . he swiped right and the app would do all the confessing for me. For both of us.

The thought of that little two-dimensional *It's a match!* firework popping up on my screen made me shiver. How amazing would that be? How *easy* would that be?

"We need a blocker!" Emily shouted from the track. "Blaine, can you lend a hand?"

"Yeah!" I shouted without lifting my head. I chewed on the inside of my cheek. Now or never.

And I swiped right.

○ ● ●

Nothing had happened.

No match. No anything. I checked Hooked multiple times

a day, but it was silent. Terrified I'd freaked Lysander out, I sent a few test IMs his way on Thursday and Friday. He responded as per normal—quick, funny, riddled with GIFs. I double-checked that my Hooked notifications were turned on and forced myself to stop checking, even if I couldn't stop thinking about it.

Was this how it ended?

Before signing off on Friday, I tested the waters one more time.

BWickers: How's Ashley?

I bit my thumbnail, knowing I was being daring. Checked over my shoulder for the vultures, but they were occupied with their own stuff. Never mind that I'd completed all my assignments two hours ago. If I appeared too leisurely, I'd get in some sort of trouble for it.

LMay: Wouldn't know. We split.

The jubilation of that confirmation melded with my fear that he'd seen my photo on Hooked and swiped left. And if he had . . . I'd have to accept it. Get over it, like Rue said. But I needed the closure of knowing he'd swiped left, which was something I hadn't considered when I'd slapped together my profile.

Maybe he hadn't been on Hooked since Wednesday. Maybe he already matched with someone else.

BWickers: Eh, she wasn't that good at escape rooms.

LMay: [GIF of a man nodding]

I waited a long minute, wondering if he might offer up more, wondering what else I could say, if I should say anything. My pulse beat hard in my wrists, chest, and neck. Holding my breath, I typed, *I'm in love with you and have been for two years.*

I stared at the message, sighed, and deleted it.

● ○ ●

"Still nothing," I whined as I let myself into Rue's basement apartment. She had a towel twisted atop her head from her shower and was painting her nails in her small kitchen. I pulled up a stool and plopped my phone, Hooked app open, between us.

Frowning, Rue put the nail polish aside, blew on her index finger, and carefully turned my phone around so she wouldn't smudge anything. A few delicate presses later, and she said, "He's not in your favorites."

I stretched forward to see the screen. "Oh. But he was. I swiped right on him." And no one else.

She frowned. Refreshed the app and checked again. "I'm pretty sure that only happens if the other person deletes their account."

"Deletes it?" Grabbing my phone, I looked longingly at the blank Favorites screen.

"How long has it been like that?" Rue asked.

"I don't know."

Her mouth twisted as she redipped her nail polish brush

into its sparkly maroon bottle. "Don't ever become a private detective."

My insides twisted. "Maybe he saw that I liked him and freaked out and deleted it."

"He can't see that you liked him unless he also likes you."

"Maybe he did it to test me." But I quickly threw that idea away. Lysander wouldn't play games. He'd also be mortified to be caught up in technology claiming he liked someone when he didn't. I turned the phone screen off.

"So much for that," I said. I went to my profile and moved to delete my account. A pop-up bubble read, *Are you sure?*

"Don't," Rue advised, not looking up from the painting of her pinky. "He might hop back on. I've deleted and reinstalled that thing more times than I can count." She shrugged. "But you should keep it for *yourself*. In case you decide to get out there again. There's a lot to choose from."

"A lot like Matthew," I mumbled.

"Hey." She waved her hand to dry her nails. "Not my fault he has a stick up his butt."

"No, it's not." I was grateful for Rue's effort, honestly. If nothing else, I'd gotten free pasta out of it. "Your nails look nice."

She grinned. "Thanks. I'm NPCing as a sorceress today at the park and thought it would add a nice touch."

If I had my LARPing knowledge straight, NPCing meant she was playing a side character today. Probably to save money.

"You should come," she offered.

I shrugged. "Maybe another time." Though running around a park with a bunch of adults in costume, hitting each other with foam swords, wasn't exactly my cup of tea.

I glanced at my phone. The Hooked *Are you sure?* pop-up bubble still waited for me.

Sighing, I hit Cancel, but didn't bother shopping around. I wasn't in the mood.

And I hadn't given up yet.

● ● ○

LYSANDER

I took the stairs up to the fifth floor; we'd gotten a help request from the executive assistant stating one of her monitors wasn't turning on. Jeff was out sick, and I'd already assigned both Artem and Kate to help out the developers, since half that department wasn't getting internet for some reason. Hadn't hired a replacement for me yet, but I had some interviews on Friday. I'd never interviewed anyone in my life and honestly wished I could delegate that too, but this was my job now, and I was going to do my job, so I'd have to get over it. Being able to read the questions from a piece of paper would help, and I reminded myself that the people coming in had no idea who I was, so there were no expectations to meet.

The elevators opened to a large reception area where Eva's enormous desk sat with its two monitors, printer, scanner, fax machine, and a giant copier behind her chair. She was a little younger than me and had replaced the old executive assistant, who retired almost a year ago.

I had a new monitor under my arm to test her connections and, worst-case scenario, to leave up here if the current one had died. She was focused on her working screen and didn't notice me until I was at the desk.

"May I?" I asked.

She glanced up at me and started. Maybe I should have been louder approaching. Or been more specific as to why I was there.

"Oh." She glanced at the monitor. "You're from IT. Yes." She scooted back.

We'd met a few times before, but I didn't point it out to her. I set the monitor down and checked the plugs from my side of the desk before coming around to her side. Hit the power button a few times. You'd be surprised how often a fix was that easy.

Not so today. So I unplugged the black monitor, moved it aside, and grabbed the new one.

"Oh wow," she said. I glanced at her as her eyes lifted up from my company badge, which hung from a lanyard around my neck. "Lysander. I know you."

I just nodded and continued my work.

"You look *way* different."

I was grateful to be busy because it gave my hands something to do and my face somewhere to be pointed.

"I mean, like, good different," she amended. "Can I see your picture?"

No was the first response in my mind, but that might make this awkward. I knew I came off as indifferent sometimes because I was quiet, and *no* might just make me sound hostile. Suppressing a sigh, I took the lanyard off my neck and handed it to her, then refocused on the monitor so I wouldn't have to see her ogling my photo.

It's a compliment, I reminded myself.

The new monitor turned on just fine. Which meant all the cords were working. I'd have to take the other one downstairs and see what was wrong with it. Or, rather, see if Artem wanted it when he was done. I had some résumés to read and a meeting at one with the developers working on the infrastructure project, which we'd pet-named Infrared for no good reason.

"Wow," Eva said. "Like *way* better. That's crazy!" she paused. "Do you want a water or something? We keep a fridge up here."

She'd never offered me a water the other times I'd been up here.

"No, thanks." I held out my hand for my lanyard. She returned it and spied the new monitor. "Oh hey! It's working! Thanks so much."

I nodded, grabbed the old monitor, and headed on my way. I took the stairs, not the elevator, hoping the shot of cardio would shake off that newfound temper of mine. *I'm sick of this. I'm so sick of this.* I should move. Start somewhere new, with no expectations . . . except I'd just gotten that promotion. My sigh echoed in the stairwell. *Maybe it'll just pass.* A couple more months, and there won't be a comparison. Maybe I should take a new employee photo.

I was halfway down the stairs, quietly boiling, when my phone rang. My screen read *MOM.*

I answered. "Yeah."

"My printer isn't working again, and I wanted to print out these book club invitations. Do you have time today?"

I sighed. "I think so."

"I'll feed you."

"That's okay."

"I'll *feed you*," she insisted.

I passed someone in the stairwell and moved over to let him through. "Do you want me to just buy you a new printer? They're not that expensive."

"No! I don't want to learn a new printer. This one works just fine."

"If it works just fine, why are you calling me?"

She sniffed. "I'll see you at six. Love you."

"Love you," I murmured, and hung up.

○ ● ●

BLAINE

I was going to do it.

Today.

I decided this Monday morning, when I passed Lysander in one of the meeting rooms on the main floor, his bearded jaw pressed against his knuckles as he watched someone present on the monitor on the wall. When my heart did that little flip that feels like it's on its own rollercoaster. When he glanced up through the glass walls and spied me, and I'd waved, and he'd nodded, and I couldn't help but think, *what if it were possible for me to get more than a nod?*

What if it *could* happen?

What if I could spend late nights talking to Lysander on the phone, or holding his hand through a park, or snuggled into him on a sofa? What if I could kiss him good night at the end of the day? What if I didn't have to, because he stayed over?

What if. What if. What if.

My brain tried to talk me out of it. It was rainy today, so I'd driven my car, but I'd still gotten wet on my way in, so my hair was frizzy. *You should wait until your hair looks nicer to tell him.* I didn't want to do it during work hours, so I would invite him to something—maybe drinks—and do it there. *If he turns you down, it's a sign. He just got a promotion, he doesn't have time for you. He didn't match you on Hooked.*

But I had to know. I had to *know.* I couldn't move on until I knew for sure. Couldn't throw my line for another fish until I was positive my bait wouldn't attract a bluefin.

I'd waited last time and lost my chance. I didn't want to lose my chance again, because how many more would the universe give me?

I talked myself through it. We weren't in the same department, so if he wasn't interested, it's not like I had to see him every day or work with him. . . . I'd just miss the instant messages that literally were the only thing keeping me sane some days. But Lysander was mature, kind, and sensitive. If he turned me down, he would be gentle. I . . . I felt safe, with him. Even if two years of hoping were to be shattered. He'd never be cruel, like the others had been. I had more confidence in that than anything else.

I was too nervous to message him that day, though after lunch he sent me that same GIF of the man with the exploding head. I smiled.

BWickers: Long day?

LMay: Everything I've heard in three hours of meetings could literally be taken care of in three emails.

BWickers: Welcome to the corporate world!
Can I get you something? A drink from the café? A
cup of smart carbs? A kitten?

LMay: [GIF of child crying]
I'm allergic to cats.

That's okay, because I don't have one, I wanted to say.
But maybe that was too forward.

But maybe I needed to be more forward.

BWickers: That's okay. I don't have one.

LMay: I noticed.

I let out a long breath and pulled up the presentation I
was formatting for one of the engineers. I was going to do it
today. I'd trained myself for six freaking months to do this,
so it wasn't a big deal. That became my mantra as every
minute ticked by: *It's not a big deal. It's not a big deal. It's
not a big deal.*

Even if he turned me down, wouldn't it be a relief to
know? To end the torture?

And if he didn't . . . wouldn't today be the literal best day
of my life, rain, Carol, and all?

I must have been nervous-drinking water, because I went
to the bathroom every thirty minutes the rest of the afternoon.
Every time I stood in front of the mirror to wash my hands,
I rehearsed the things I could say. Maybe a smidge of liquid
courage would help. I would definitely ask him to drinks.

On my last pep session, I passed Nora on the way out of

the bathroom. "You're peeing more than I am." She chuckled. Paused. "You're not pregnant, are you?"

I rolled my eyes. "Literally impossible. Just hydrated."

She high-fived me and went in to do her business.

I checked my watch. 4:45 p.m.

I was going to do this.

● ○ ●

I was prepared to hardcore stalk Lysander to talk with him after work—I didn't want to ask him out on instant messenger. I was prepared to work overtime if he ended up working overtime, because I was pumped and eager and ready to go. About the same way one is pumped and eager and ready to go at the entrance of an adult-only haunted house, when you haven't quite started the tour but it's too late to turn back.

So yes, I was terrified. Hands-shaking-over-keyboard terrified. And I did whatever I could to keep my mind off it. I even chatted up Carol about her cats in the elevator. Then I sauntered over to our receptionist and asked her about her day, her last weekend, and her future weekend—

And then Lysander came down the stairs. He always took the stairs now. He headed straight for the doors, not noticing me. He had a laptop bag slung over his shoulder and his employee ID tucked into his back pocket; the lanyard swung back and forth with his stride. It caught my eye, and I looked at his butt and smiled when I thought about the moon tattoo, and I garnered a sliver more courage.

"That sounds like fun," I told the receptionist and waved. "I've got to head. Don't work too hard."

She grinned. "Never do."

Lysander reached the doors just as I turned around. I strode in his direction, one hand a death grip on the strap of my purse, the other opening and closing at my side, trying to dispense some of the nervous energy eating my insides like termites. My pursuit was silent—I was wearing ballet flats and nothing with that satisfactory heel echo that I swear every business woman loves.

I was going to do this.

Lysander drove a blue Camry, and I spotted it just before spotting him. He was parked on the east side of the lot; I was on the south. I picked up my pace a little. He reached the trunk and popped it open.

"Lysander!" I called.

He turned toward me. A small smile pulled on his lips—good sign. I quickened my pace as much as I could without running. The last thing I needed was a red and sweaty face while I did this.

"Heading home?" he asked. He sounded tired.

"Maybe." My heart thudded like a marching bass drum in my chest, and it reverberated all the way down to my heels. So much so I was sure my entire body pulsated. I tucked some hair behind my ear, then noticed my hand was shaking and quickly dropped it. *Cool, calm, collected. You are cool, calm, and collected.*

"I was wondering"—my voice didn't shake too much, thank goodness—"if you wanted to go get a drink with me? Just at Limon down the street. I'll drive. And pay." I waggled my eyebrows in mock enticement.

That small smile lingered. He looked tired too—but of course he was. It was the end of the workday and it was a Tuesday. Tuesdays sucked almost as much as Mondays did.

"Honestly, that sounds nice." He chucked his laptop into his trunk. "But my mom's expecting me for dinner. Her stone-age printer is malfunctioning again."

"Oh." The termites crawled into my stomach. Crap. Crap. Crap. My entire plan hinged on us getting drinks. Of being semi-alone and maybe even slightly buzzed. "Did she try turning it off and on again?"

He snorted and closed his trunk. "If she turns it off, I'm not sure it will turn back on."

I laughed, but it was more a nervous laugh than anything. "Maybe tomorrow."

He nodded. "Maybe."

But I was amped up. I was going to do this today, wasn't I? This nervous energy was about to send me to the ER.

We were in the parking lot, and no one was close by . . . this was semi-alone, wasn't it?

I was going to lose my nerve. I waited last time and I'd lost my chance.

Lost my chance.

He turned for the driver's side door.

"I like you!" I blurted, and felt heat roll up my back and sting my cheeks. He just froze, keys in hand. He didn't say anything, and the silence made me feel naked, so I amended, "I really like you. Like, I-want-to-date-you like you."

There it was. Vomited and sitting on the asphalt between us. And if I thought my bass-drum pulse was loud before, it was damn right deafening now.

He kneaded his keys in his hands and I wondered if I should apologize for saying—

"*Now* you like me." His voice was so quiet I almost didn't hear it over the traffic on the street.

"I do . . . I mean, what?" The termites chewed and chewed and chewed. "No, I've liked you for a really long time—"

"God, Blaine." He clutched the keys in one hand and rubbed his eyes with another, like he had a headache. "I thought you of all people would be different."

Nausea assaulted me. I didn't understand. I thought I'd pictured every possible scenario for how this would go, but I hadn't. "What do you mean, different?"

He shook his head. The fatigue in his eyes increased, as did the lines on his forehead. He looked skyward, like offering a silent prayer. "Like you weren't just one more shallow woman who finally decided I was worth something."

I reeled back like he'd slapped me. He *had* slapped me. Something in my mind, and another something in my heart, cracked from the blow. "Shallow? *Excuse me?*" I'd been called a lot of things in my life, but *shallow* had never been one of them.

"You're excused." He grabbed the handle of the door.

"Do you think this is a joke?" Razor blades edged my voice. "Or do you think you're such a cat's meow now that I don't deserve to be taken seriously?"

He paused long enough to look at me, and I was struck at how *angry* his expression was. I'd never seen him angry. Not like this. "Guess not. Bye, Blaine."

I gaped at him. My eyes stung. As he sat down, and before he closed the door, I snapped, "I didn't realize San Jose had turned you into a massive asshole."

I didn't wait to see his response. I fled. I marched like a soldier on the warpath to my car, nearly jogging by the time I reached it. Jerked my driver's side door open. Chucked my purse onto the passenger seat. Shoved my key into the ignition and turned it—the engine revved, then choked. It must have felt the heat of my wrath, however, because when I stomped on the brake and turned it again, the engine started.

With a death grip on the steering wheel, I backed out of the spot and took the closest exit onto the road, even though it was a right-turn only and my house was left. I drove, way faster than the speed limit, until I caught up with the car in front of me.

Piece by piece, I started to shatter. My vision blurred. My hands shook. My breathing turned hard, yet I couldn't get enough air.

Half a mile down the street, I pulled into a Dairy Queen parking lot. Cut in front of the drive-through lane and parked in the farthest available slot, by some tall hedges laced with spiderwebs.

I stared at the little horn signal on my steering wheel. Stared at it for a few seconds or a few hours, I couldn't tell.

The tears came first, one after another, ruining my mascara and dribbling down my face. So fast that when I wiped one away, two more replaced it. I checked my purse for tissues, and of course I was out. Fortunately, past-Blaine had stashed a napkin in the glove box.

After the first sob ripped up my throat, there was no going back. So I pushed my chair all the way back, hunched over, and cried into a flimsy brown napkin, trying to keep my mouth closed to stifle the sound, because the last thing I wanted was a do-gooder in the parking lot knocking on my window and asking if I was okay.

I was not okay.

I thought he was different. I pressed the napkin in harder and shivered with another sob. *Let me down easy. What a joke.*

And apparently that's all I'd been to him. A joke.

Was I that disgusting? Was I that *deluded*?

Obviously, I was. That was the consensus, wasn't it? Greg, Ryan, Chad, Lysander . . . like the world was shouting at me, *Why do you even try?*

I should have listened to Rue. I should have just moved on. Maybe she knew all along and didn't want to hurt my feelings. I should have taken her hint.

But I thought he'd be different. I really, stupidly thought . . .

All my fantasies cracked like overcooked peanut brittle, and tasted just as bitter. Each one made me feel more idiotic. Each one forged new tears and triggered new sobs. I had to forfeit my napkin to a running nose and had to use my shirt for everything else. What a mess.

Shallow.

That word rang through my head in an endless cycle, edged in Lysander's baritone voice, condemning me over and over and over again. *Shallow. Shallow. Shallow.*

Asshole.

I cried until I had nothing left to cry. Until my throat hurt and my mouth was dry and my eyes were swollen, red, and scratchy. I stayed in my car, hiccupping, staring at the hedges until I felt like I could drive without getting myself killed.

This time, the car started on the first try. Huh, look at that. I'd missed rush hour.

Shriveled and empty, I drove myself home.

Chapter 8

MY BRAIN AND body didn't know what to feel.

I bounced between confusion, anger, and despair, sometimes all three at once. It was world-turning. Maybe because I'd forgotten how utterly miserable this feeling had been the last few times this happened. Maybe it was because I'd never dedicated this much time to a guy, and two years of my life seemed wasted. Maybe it was because I really, actually believed I loved Lysander.

Or had. I wasn't sure. It was hard to feel love when everything else inside and outside of me was a hot bubbling mess. Hot mess enough that I called in sick Wednesday. The last thing I needed was to break down at my desk with its non-privacy low cubicle walls, or worse, run into Lysander.

For being the object of my desire for so long, it was disconcerting that he was now the last person in the world I wanted to see. I'd rather have tea with my backstabbing ex-friend Monica, the catalyst of terrible confession explosion number two, than risk passing Mr. May in the hallway.

I didn't tell Rue. I didn't tell anyone. I just came home, executed a terrible parking job in the driveway, and went straight to my bedroom. Then to the kitchen, where I consumed literally everything with a high calorie count and took a sick sense of pride that none if it was smart carbs. Then to the shower.

I think Rue might have heard me sobbing in the shower, because she was waiting for me in the living room after that. And I stupidly couldn't explain without crying, so despite lying four feet away from her, I texted her as many details as I could stomach to share.

It took forever to spell that word. *S-h-a-l-l-o-w.*

"Good!" she exclaimed when I texted what I'd said to him before storming off. "Because he *is* an asshole! He's a poisonous douchebag who thinks he's God's gift to mankind! Why are men such *jerks*?"

That was just a sample of her rant. Because Rue could get very . . . colorful . . . when she was angry.

It didn't make me feel much better, but I appreciated the support.

I slept a lot on Wednesday. Cried, then got angry at myself for crying over a man, which I guess made me not feminist or something, and then I'd feel guilty, which would make me cry, which made me think of why I'd been crying in the first place, and then I'd be sad and cry even more. It was a horrible cycle.

I'd take a year of PMS over a day of that horrible, stupid cycle.

By Wednesday night, after a lot of cold spoons on my eyes, I dressed and drove to derby. I wasn't going to miss a game because of a broken heart and shattered pride. I didn't carpool with Rue. I drove my bike. Revved it loudly and broke every speed limit, because it made me feel better to do so. Kept the visor on my helmet up so the wind could beat me into sanity.

I might as well have stayed home. Overeager on the track, I got sent to the penalty box twice, then ejected from the game entirely. So while Rue led our team to victory, I turned a stack of tumbling mats in the back room into a punching bag and went at it until my knuckles bled.

Rue made me dinner that night because she's an angel of mercy. She said nothing about the Band-Aids on my knuckles.

I considered taking Thursday off too, but IO Masters wasn't the most generous with paid time off, so I dragged myself to work the next day, my hair in a ponytail because I didn't wash it, and I honestly didn't care if the undercut and the blue chunks got me a dress code violation.

No one, even Carol, said anything about it. Probably because I didn't exactly hide the fact that I was a simmering dark lord leaking shadows, waiting to strike.

My instant messenger flashed, and my heart panged so hard I nearly puked. But it wasn't Lysander—it was Nora.

NPatterson: You okay?

BWickers: I'm alive.

NPatterson: Want to talk about it?

BWickers: Sorry, I really don't.

Nora, bless her, didn't pester. And when she came back from lunch, she set a slice of cheesecake from the café quietly on the desk beside the document I was copy editing and left. The act made my eyes water, but I managed to keep the rest in. Honestly, my thirty-six-hour-long pity party had really sugared me out, but I ate the cheesecake anyway, because it wasn't a smart carb, and I felt like it gave me some sort of spiteful victory.

I just . . . didn't get it. Lysander and I had been friends for so long. He'd come to my birthday party. He's given me a really thoughtful gift, which was currently locked away in the bottom of my filing cabinet. He knew me. I knew him. And yet . . .

Maybe he'd been having a *really* bad day, but if that were the case . . . wouldn't he have apologized by now? And even if he was in a sour mood, wouldn't he have the presence of mind, the emotional intelligence, not to take it out on me, when I was in such a vulnerable state?

I blinked rapidly and turned back to my work, desperate to splice sentences and correct spelling. I plugged in my headphones and blasted jazz to keep my thoughts on literally anything but Lysander. For the most part, it worked.

And I didn't see Lysander at all Thursday, or Friday. I didn't see him in a meeting room, I didn't run into him in the hallway, and his name didn't pop up in my instant messenger.

And given that I didn't have a good reason to stay at IO Masters anymore, I spent all of Saturday submitting my résumé all over the Wasatch Front.

And a few copies made it up to Washington.

• • ○

LYSANDER

I glanced at my instant messenger while skewering a carrot at my new desk. I don't know why I did. It'd been quiet for days. My staff didn't use it—if they needed to talk to me, they just walked over.

I wasn't surprised. I didn't expect anything. But old habits were hard to bury, so my eyes strayed there again and again.

Didn't matter, or so I told myself. So I muted it and all my social media, including Hooked, which I'd reinstalled yesterday but hadn't used. I needed a break from the world. I needed to remember who I was and not the box everyone wanted to put me in.

Even Blaine liked that box. And for some reason, it felt like a betrayal. Hurt more than the others.

And I told myself I didn't care.

○ • •

BLAINE

Next Tuesday morning, a day filled with filtered air and the light scent of someone's overcooked Pop-Tart flowing from the break room, Carol meandered into the little hallway between all of our cubicles without word, just stood there, expecting her presence to be seen.

That's how we started our morning meetings. Every. Single. Day.

Kristi, another writer, followed after, holding a printed

itinerary in her hand. I hurried and saved the file I'd been working on for a whole two minutes, then grabbed the cardigan I kept at work because even in September, the office was always a few degrees too cold.

I sauntered over and leaned against the edge of my cubicle wall while everyone else assembled. Sometimes I made small talk while this phenomenon happened, if only to be friendly. Lately, I hadn't felt like it.

Nora, whose cubicle was the farthest and who presently walked the slowest, was the last to arrive, waddling with one hand on her enormous stomach. IO Masters offered six weeks of maternity leave, but Nora wasn't going to use it until she absolutely needed it. She'd mentioned once that six weeks wasn't very long when a newborn was involved.

Carol checked her watch and frowned, apparently disappointed that we were starting at 9:02 and not 9:00 sharp. Or, perhaps, she was disappointed that she couldn't write up Nora for making us late, because being pregnant wasn't against company policy.

I wondered if I'd get any callbacks on those résumés I'd sent out this week.

"Midwest conference is this weekend," Carol said with all the enthusiasm of a woken mummy. "So we need to start on the Pacific conference." She looked at Kristi. "Do we have everything uploaded on those thumb drives?"

She nodded. "Everything but Max's presentations."

Carol glanced to me. "Aren't those on your docket?"

I held in a sigh. "Yes. I sent them to you for review last Thursday."

She raised an eyebrow. "I didn't get them."

She did, she just hadn't gotten around to them. But Carol didn't like to make mistakes. "They're in your inbox. I sent them in a zip around two o'clock."

Shrugging one shoulder, she said, "Resend them."

I gave her a thumbs-up. Though I honestly wanted to present a different finger.

"Next," Carol moved on, "IO Masters is building an internal infrastructure system called Infrared to help with customer servicing. They need a writer to put the software they're building into lay terms for everyone—there needs to be a set of internal and external documentation. It'll be a sizable project, and with the Pacific conference coming up, we can only spare one writer. I just sent the latest case studies to Blaine, so"—she clicked her tongue and thought for a moment—"Nora, I'm going to assign you to take it on."

"Okay." Nora sounded hesitant. "How long of a project is it?"

Carol sighed. "I have no idea. Month or two, maybe."

Nora exchanged an awkward glanced with me. "Not to be the problem child, but I'm due on October tenth."

And today was the nineteenth of September.

"Oh." Carol stared at Nora deadpan, like she was using psychic powers to persuade the baby to come at a later date.

And then I realized something that made goose bumps rise on my arms and back.

Wouldn't big infrastructure involve IT? And be run by the product manager over IT? The position Lysander recently got promoted to?

My stomach dropped so hard it switched places with my uterus. *Oh please, not me not me not me not me not me.*

"We'll have Blaine do it, then."

"I, uh." I sounded like a genuine toad and cleared my throat. Heat flashed through my torso. "Those case studies really weren't in good shape—"

"Kristi's going to the Midwest conference, yes?" Carol glanced at Kristi, who nodded. And Carol, being Carol, just started walking back to her desk, like we would all just accept her directives and there'd be nothing left to discuss. "So we'll give the case studies to Nora and see how much she can get done before her leave."

My mouth went dry. Please, please let Nora's water break *right now*. I changed my birthday wish. I wanted Nora's water to break *right now* so I'd *have* to do those case studies—

Her pants remained dry.

"And then we'll switch them back to you," Carol went on. "You might have to pull overtime."

"Overtime?" I repeated. When one was a salaried employee, overtime was the worst.

Overtime . . . with Lysander.

But maybe he'd delegate someone else, like Jeff or Kate, to work on it with me . . .

"And who is over the project?" My fingers grew cold.

"Aaron Kempton," she answered.

My posture crumbled. "Aaron doesn't work here anymore."

"Oh," Nora chimed in, "it would be Lysander May. That works out—Blaine knows him really well." She smiled at me, and my expression must have been something, because her smile vanished and her eyes went wide. I couldn't blame her. She didn't know. No one did.

And even if they did, Carol wouldn't care.

My mind raced as I scrambled for an excuse to get out of this. Couldn't I go to the Midwest conference instead? But I wasn't prepped for it, and Kristi's tickets were already purchased. Could I have Nora's baby? Nope, not possible. Could I fake mono and stay home for the entire project? Not enough PTO.

Could I beg on my hands and knees, grabbing at Carol's dress pants and begging her to do it for me? But she was a supervisor; she couldn't be assigned elsewhere. And there was no way on God's green planet Carol would ever allow herself to do anything she didn't want to do, and she definitely didn't want to do this. She was already zombied-out in front of her screens.

Or I could quit. I could just quit, right then, right there. Not bother giving my two weeks. Just storm off and say goodbye.

But who knew how quickly I'd get another job, even with my résumés out in the market? And I had a mortgage to pay.

Damn all of this to hell.

"Okay." It came out like a whisper. Like the final word of a criminal sentenced to death row.

Because in truth, I might actually rather die than work with Lysander. I wasn't ready to see him again, let along be in a room with him and talk to him and be at his disposal.

Carol blinked back into human mode. "There's a meeting in room 205 at one o'clock today. You'll need to attend."

I gripped the cubicle wall, sure I'd crumble if I didn't. Fantastic. Four whole hours to prepare myself to sit in a room with the guy who demeaned me and threw me away like so much garbage. Carol might as well have taken a shiv and shanked me through my diaphragm.

I crawled back to my desk. Dropped into my chair. My eyes burned, but I had enough resolve to keep tears at bay.

Plugging in my earbuds, I turned on classical music and dropped my head into my hands, breathing deeply.

When that didn't make me feel better, I switched the playlist to metal.

Chapter 9

PLEASE BE A *big meeting. Please be a big meeting.* If there were a ton of people at that meeting, I could tuck myself in the back, avoid eye contact, and get out of there quickly. Take notes and go. *Please be a big meeting.*

There were three other people in the meeting room when I showed up a minute late. My eyes, of course, went straight to Lysander, sitting at the head of the table. The vision of him physically hurt. Like someone with long but dull nails reached through my chest and ripped out my heart to use as a hacky sack. I pulled my eyes away and saw the head developer and the vice president in the other seats. Despite it looking awkward, I took a seat at the far end of the table, leaving seven empty chairs between me and the others on one side, and six on the other.

I kept my eyes on the yellow notebook I'd brought with me. Heard the buzz of the projector as it turned on. Glanced up as Lysander stood to present.

His eyes met mine. For a second he looked startled, then just . . . cold.

Jerk. I bandaged the cool spike of humiliation and hurt in hot anger and glared at the screen.

He introduced Infrared via a short PowerPoint presentation. I tried to keep my eyes on the slides and not on him as my metaphorical chest wound festered. He only stuttered once, which surprised me. He really had gained a lot more confidence since coming back from California.

Good for him, I thought in the most sarcastic manner I could. *Makes it easier to shatter people that way.*

I wondered if he'd been cruel to Ashley too, and felt simultaneously sorry for her and a sudden kinship with her. Letting my eyes unfocus, I pictured old Lysander up there, with his clean-shaven face and soft chin. Old Lysander wouldn't have acted that way . . . right?

What was I missing?

Lysander, thankfully, sat down. I swiveled my chair so the vice president's body shielded most of my vision of him.

"The CEO wants this leg of the project done in *four* weeks," the VP said. "I know it's steep, but we want something the salesforce can show off."

The head developer sighed. "You're killing my guys."

"We'll cater dinner for them," he offered. "Make it worth their while."

I wanted to ask if they'd bring in dinners for me, if I was going to be working overtime, but the words didn't make it past my teeth.

The VP checked his watch. "I have another meeting to attend, but I expect you guys will do well on your own." He clapped Lysander on the shoulder. Lysander probably hated that. Good. I dropped my eyes as the VP walked to the glass door and let himself out.

"This will be an evening project for sure," the developer said, and sighed again. "All right. I'll get the boys assigned."

I knew at least one developer was a woman, but again, I didn't say anything.

The developer moved to stand, so I did too, only to have Lysander say, "I take it you're assigned for documentation."

His voice was deadpan but still rang knife sharp in my ears.

I lowered myself to my seat. The developer missed my pleading look as he, too, left the room.

I grimaced inwardly. "Last I checked, that was my job, so."

"I have a few other projects"—Lysander looked at his notes, not me—"so this will be an evening event for me too."

"So I was warned. Overtime." My tone wasn't any lighter than his.

He sighed and sat up. "The sooner we work on this, the faster it will be done, so let's start tomorrow. Five o'clock, IT."

I prickled as I realized something. "I can't tomorrow." I had a derby game. "Can we start Thursday?"

Now he looked at me. Darkly, tiredly, just like he had in the parking lot last week, and the starkness of it made my face heat, like he was dismissing me and telling me I was shallow all over again. "Why can't you do tomorrow?"

"I have a game."

"Game?"

"A derby game. I'm in roller derby. I'm a blocker." He knew this. Or maybe he didn't. Maybe he actually had ignored everything I'd told him over the last two and half years.

He glowered. "What's more important, your job or your roller skates?"

I gaped at him. Did he really just say that to me? And in that dark, condescending voice?

This wasn't Lysander. This was Bizarro Lysander. He'd been Superman and now he'd morphed into some sort of villainous equivalent. And I was fresh out of kryptonite.

I didn't respond, so he just picked up his papers and stood. "See you tomorrow."

And I just sat there, gaping at him, giving him the finger underneath the table as he sauntered out, not glancing my way a second time.

● ○ ●

This was the actual worst.

My neck was starting to hurt from how tense I was, sitting in this oversized cubicle in IT, my back to Lysander. And even though I couldn't see him with our computers opposite of one another, I felt his presence like one feels a space heater cranked too high. I hadn't taken a full breath since arriving *two hours ago*.

Because heaven forbid, I work at my own desk. Nope, this was the VP's idea, may he rot in tech hell. It made us more efficient, since Infrared was so new and we needed to communicate. And granted, he was right—I'd already had half a dozen questions since dragging myself down here at a quarter after five, after getting myself a sandwich at the café. But I'd directed as many as I could to Frank, the head developer, who got lucky and resided in the cubicle next to us.

Karma was messing with me. I'm the one who convinced Lysander to take a chance on this job, and now I got to wallow in the intense awkwardness of it. I swear I could feel his utter dislike for me whispering in my hair like so many spiders.

Shivering, I clicked to the next slide of the poorly made PowerPoint I'd been given on a thumb drive. There was a reason all public presentations went through the technical writers before leaving the company. Not only did we make them match the company's branding, but we made them make sense. For example, this slide had *fifteen* bullet points on it, and the font was painfully small to make them all fit. In a presentation, no one would be able to read them. And they weren't even parallel.

It took all my inner strength to just read through the slide and not *fix the bullets*. I'd never get out of here if I edited this thing instead of translating it into a rough-draft user guide. And turning random bullet points and a smattering of notes into a user guide was not easy, and given that it was past the end of the day, my brain recoiled at every letter I typed.

My phone buzzed again. I kept it in my lap so it wouldn't vibrate off the table. I had two ongoing conversations to-night—the first with my mom, so I could vent, and the second with Rue, who was keeping me apprised of the game. The game that had started thirty minutes ago. The game I was supposed to be in, but hey, apparently, I was the only person here who cared about that.

This one was from my mom.

Mom: I'll send you a pie.

I pushed my tongue against the roof of my mouth to keep from snorting. Didn't want to get caught by my new after-hours boss.

Me: It'll be gross by the time it gets here.

Mom: Then I'll come down and make it myself.

My heart shrank.

Me: I wish.

The phone buzzed in my hands—text from Rue.

Rue: It's like we're not even trying to block.

I cringed. We were playing the Pleasant Graves tonight, arguably the weakest team within five hundred miles. I texted back.

Me: Just wait until you're up.

Then I shoved my phone between my thighs, returned to the presentation, and pulled up the notes for the slide. Read through them and typed them up in clear English on the word processor. Then I paused. Sighed.

"Is it *on* or *in* the multilevel cells?"

Lysander's chair squeaked ever so faintly as he turned. "What?"

"Here is says *in*"—I pointed to the slide without glancing

back at him—"and here it says *on*." I pointed to the notes. "Which is it?"

A pause. "Does it matter?"

The question grated on me. If I'd asked Frank, it probably wouldn't have as much. But it was Lysander and I was missing a game because he went bizarro, so it grated. "I don't know. Does the user guide making sense matter?"

He got off his chair. I still refused to look at him, but he came close, hovering over my shoulder to read the stupidly small bullet points, and my spine morphed into steel. I hated how close he was, and I hated that I actually could feel his warmth like he was a literal space heater and that he smelled like L'Homme cologne, and I hated that despite everything, his closeness made my pulse skip and my face heat, and I was very grateful I wasn't facing him.

Stop it, I begged myself. *We are so over this.*

Apparently not.

"I think it's *in*." He leaned back and strode to the edge of the cubicle, giving me a chance to breathe. "Frank, when we're talking about bit memory storage, it's *in* the MLC, right?"

"Uh . . . sure."

I rolled my eyes and bolded the word in the document. I'd check our style guide later. "Thanks," I offered half-heartedly.

And . . . that was it. There was nothing interesting whatsoever to report. I plowed ahead, ignoring the computer-headache blooming behind my eyes and the chair-butt eating my backside, and I worked, trying to get through this stupid presentation so I could go home and, I don't know, maybe have time to do something relaxing before I had to go to bed and repeat all of this tomorrow.

Right now, I really hated my job.

I had just blessedly finished my work when I got another text from Rue.

Rue: 75 to 56. We lost.

I stormed out of IO Masters without a goodbye to anyone, relishing the sputtering muffler of my motorcycle as I blazed my way home.

* * ○

LYSANDER

"You're quiet, man," Jose said as he rolled a handful of dice. We had a battle map for our latest campaign sprawled out on the table, along with all of our character sheets. We'd just leveled up, which was always fun when it came to battles, but I just wasn't feeling it tonight. So far, the new promotion was going well; I felt I had a good handle on it, minus the interviews I had to start conducting. But work had sucked the soul out of me this week, and I guess the residual stress was spilling into the weekend too.

"He's always quiet," Mark, our game master, said. "What're your numbers?"

"Sixteen and eighteen."

"The eighteen hits."

"More quiet than usual, then," Jose corrected as he dealt

damage to the werewolf that had sprung upon us, represented by a gray floral gem on the board. "What's up?"

I frowned, rolling a twenty-sided die around my palm, waiting for my turn. "Nothing."

Will, next to me, asked, "Your dad again?"

"No." While my father was often a source of stress—and not just because of his health—in truth, I couldn't pinpoint exactly what was chafing me tonight. I kneaded my thoughts like I kneaded the d20 in my palm. Work was exhausting. Being a manager was exhausting. My dad was also exhausting.

Blaine was exhausting.

I didn't know why. She did all the work I asked her to do, and while a veiled complaint slipped out here and there, it wasn't that big of a deal. But being around her, being quiet, not knowing what to say . . . maybe that was what made it so exhausting.

I missed her. I hadn't so much as sent her a GIF for a week and a half, and . . . I don't know. Reaching out to her, even just on the work IM, was often the highlight of my day. I could literally message her anything. Work stuff, movie stuff, even game stuff, though she wasn't so much into role-play.

I rethought that afternoon in the parking lot. Retraced what I'd said. I hadn't been that harsh, had I?

Well, she'd called me an asshole, so maybe I was forgetting something. Opening my hand, I frowned at the dice there.

"Ly, you're up," Mark said.

I rolled my dice, missed. Drank a potion, and the game moved on to Will.

Maybe I shouldn't have said anything. But you can't exactly *not* say something when someone blurts out that they suddenly like you. It's one thing when it's a Hooked or Facebook message—it was entirely different when it was in person.

And suddenly this woman I really liked, who I trusted, who I didn't stutter around, became someone else. This image of her sitting on my couch, laughing at my old photos, ingrained itself into my brain. Thoughts of not being enough sucked me through the asphalt. Because if I had been enough *before*, she would have said something then.

I got it. I got that physical attraction was important. But I also didn't think fat was some ultimate deciding factor in physical attraction.

Maybe I was being too harsh. Maybe I should give her a break. Had her timing been different . . . I mean, if she'd told me she liked me right when I got back from California, before Ashley and all the Hooked girls and the Facebook messages, what would I have said? Or if she had told me before I got home. Or before I left . . .

I wouldn't have believed her. Or maybe I would have, but I would have questioned everything and anything every time I was around her. The way I questioned everything and anything now. It was immobilizing.

But I trust Blaine, don't I? I chewed on the inside of my lip. I did. Or I used to.

I sighed and pulled my character sheet over. My turn was coming around again, but the stats blurred into one gray mass. I'd deleted Hooked again, then downloaded it yet again today at lunch, but I hadn't done a thing with it. I thought about updating my photo to one from before, not that I had a lot—I'd never liked having my picture taken. Then maybe, if I matched with someone . . . maybe it would be like reverse catfishing. But the thought of *that* made me feel so pompous. And honestly . . . would I even match with anyone?

I didn't know. I'd never tried online dating until California. It'd always freaked me out a little.

I let out a long breath. I got that I could use more self-love. There was actually a section on that in my nutrition counseling. And I did feel a little more confident now. But my ego was on the fritz. I hadn't yo-yoed this hard since . . . forever.

I rolled the dice and landed six bludgeoning damage on the werewolf.

The battle took an obscenely long time, and I was really tired, so we called the game an hour early. I assured my friends I was fine as they headed out. Then I retreated to my bathroom, brushed my teeth, washed my face. The usual. Hopefully I'd feel better after a long night's rest.

I stared at myself in the mirror. I'd lost more weight this last month; I was getting close to graduating my program. I pinched some of the looser skin on my hips.

We have matching stretch marks.

I sighed and went to my room, not bothering to turn on the light. Sat on the edge of my bed. Moved to plug in my phone, then paused. Opened Hooked.

I scrolled through a few women. All of them seemed fine. Some of them had decent profiles. I just couldn't bring myself to swipe right. Maybe I was too tired. Maybe I—

My thumb froze over my screen. Over her name: *Blaine.*

That was her, smiling at the camera and holding up an unbaked pie.

Something about that smile hurt. Hurt like I'd spent the

day puking, or had unbelievable heartburn. Hurt in a way oddly familiar, like I knew that kind of pain once but had since become numb to it.

Blaine smiled at me. That was the first thing I'd noticed about her, when she came to IO Masters. She smiled at me even though she didn't know who I was. Even though I was quiet and awkward and a stranger to her. And she kept smiling at me, like we were old friends, until we became friends. Until it was really easy to smile back.

But Blaine smiled at everyone. Which was a good thing, really. But I used to sit here and wish she'd only smile at me.

I still wished she'd only smile at me. Maybe things would have been different, in the parking lot. Maybe I would have gotten the courage to approach her before . . .

Subtle arrows on either side of the screen reminded me that I needed to swipe. Left, or right. No, or yes.

I stared at her face a moment longer before turning my phone off.

In the morning, I realized I'd forgotten to plug it in.

Chapter 10

BLAINE

I STOOD IN front of my mirror in my underwear, looking at myself. Really looking at myself.

My last derby bruise was fading on my thigh, which made it a gnarly green shade that would look attractive on nothing. I had a healthy dose of cellulite on my thighs, and though I knew *everyone* had cellulite, I examined it a little too long. Sucked my stomach in, let it out. Sucked it in again and turned to the side. Rubbed at old stretch marks like I could clean them from my skin. Tightened my bra straps to bring the girls a little higher. Poked at all the places that carried a little extra.

I didn't do this. Stare at myself in the mirror and pick away at all the stupid little things that society made into stupid little things. I'd stopped after the giardia thing, because I knew it never made me happy, so why do it? The same reason I stayed away from that stupid YouTube video and my old friends' social media accounts. Why do it if it was only going to make me miserable?

But there was this nagging part of my brain that wanted it. Like it was hungry, and my self-esteem was what it fed on. Like today was just a good day to hate myself. To figure out why I wasn't enough for people.

That wasn't fair. I was plenty enough for plenty of people. It wasn't like I didn't have family or friends. I wasn't a thirty-year-old virgin or anything. But with every stretch mark I poked, every fat pocket I prodded, their names spun through my mind on a relentless wheel. *Greg, Ryan, Chad, Lysander. Greg, Ryan, Chad, Lysander.*

Which made me start wondering, if I were skinnier, or if my nose were different, or if my teeth were whiter . . . would they have liked me back?

Or maybe it was my personality that was so repulsive.

Or maybe it was both.

Groaning aloud, I tore myself from the mirror and got dressed. Paused, then put something else on, something cuter, despite the fact that today was Sunday and I had no plans. But I wanted to feel good about myself. I usually felt good about myself. This was stupid. I knew it was stupid.

I just wished I could feel it too.

○ ● ●

NPatterson: I saw that to-go box. Café? You're not working late again, are you?

BWickers: Yep. Again. They're ruthless.

NPatterson: The CEO is ruthless! Is this another 60-hr week?

BWickers: [Crying emoji]
Can I have your baby for you? Please? I'll let you
keep half your maternity leave.

NPatterson: Oh honey, believe me, that would not
be a fair trade.

Sighing, I closed out all my documents, ensuring they
were all saved with today's date, and logged out of the system.
It was two minutes after five. I clutched my cooling Reuben in
its plastic clamshell that would ensure it was nice and soggy
by the time I got around to eating it. As I headed toward
the third floor, my legs slowly morphed into family-reunion
coolers, packed with soda and ice, heavy and cold. Like my
body would do anything to avoid going into that cubicle
again. Maybe even another round of giardia.

Maybe not.

It really wasn't as bad as the first couple of days. I was getting used to the quiet drag of overtime, and the silent stiffness
dear Frank was completely oblivious to. And I was prepared
to put in even more overtime if it meant getting out of here
early on Wednesday for my next derby game. It wasn't fair
to the team to leave them hanging. Not to toot my own horn,
but I was a good blocker. No one could skate by these hips.

Lysander had asked me what was more important, my job
or my roller skates. The right answer was my job. The real
answer was my skates. But roller derby didn't pay the bills,
so I kept my mouth shut.

I had a phone interview with an electrical solutions company in Ogden during my lunch break tomorrow. Which I
would take in the comfortably cramped privacy of the supply

closet. Hopefully, it would go well. It would feel weird to leave "Happy Valley," but it might be for the better.

And I'd be an hour closer to home, and my mom. Which still made for an eleven-hour drive, assuming good weather.

I got there before Lysander and Frank did, so I set up my workstation, plugged in my laptop, took a bite of Reuben, and looked at my itinerary. Today I was reading through my latest transcriptions and trying to make them into understandable English. My goal was to make it understandable for anyone at a client company, not just the engineers and developers.

It was a slightly monumental task.

I printed out the document and was reviewing it with a red pen in one hand, sandwich in the other, when Lysander came in.

Apparently, some caterpillars had crawled into my stomach during breakfast, because they all hatched into overeager butterflies right at that moment.

I started swinging a proverbial flyswatter, never taking my eyes from my work.

Lysander dropped a packet beside my abandoned clamshell. "This is from Peter downstairs. Answers to your questions."

Questions I had written down Thursday night before heading home. I glanced over and frowned at the chicken scratch. "Great, now all I need is an interpreter."

I thought I caught a tick of a smile on the corner of his mouth as Lysander turned for his computer. What, was I funny again now? I guess a joke was a joke, even if the delivery system was unsavory.

Shallow.

I bit down on a sigh, and the air escaped through my nose. To my surprise, the thought didn't invoke rage. Just . . . sadness. Like I'd been successful in my butterfly smashing and now I just stood there, surrounded by colorful, lifeless corpses.

Trying to focus on work, I scooted over to the chicken scratch. This was essentially my key for simplifying the user guide, but I had to decode it first. Made me, ironically, think of the escape room. Of Lysander sitting beside me while I pieced together that jumbled alphabet.

How would that night have gone, if Ashley hadn't been there? Or if I'd simply not cared? If I'd said, *I like you. Like I-want-to-date-you like you* in the hall by my front door, after showing him my tattoo and laughing at his, in that close private space surrounded by the noise of people who cared about me. Would he still have called me shallow, or though I was "different," whatever that meant? Or would he have said, *I like you too*, or *Maybe we can work something out*, or even, *I'm so sorry, Blaine. I just don't feel the same way*.

It would have hurt massively, but I'd have taken *I don't feel the same way* over *shallow*.

I glanced over my shoulder at him. He'd gotten a haircut. It was still long on top—longer than it had ever been before San Jose. He still wore his beard, and I was so used to it now, I think it would startle me if he shaved it. It looked good on him. His blazer looked good on him—it was simple and hugged his shoulders, which I'd always loved. Shoulders I'd fantasized lying my head on while we watched *Willow*. Did the blazer hide another graphic tee? I hadn't noticed.

Did that make me shallow, if I thought he was cute? But

what did he expect? Attractiveness had always been part of the romancing equation, and he was an idiot if he thought it didn't.

Or did he prefer women like Ashley? Rope-thin, tan, blond-haired women who probably had a million Instagram followers and eyelashes that could open doors.

Or was it that girls like Ashley also thought *he* was cute?

Now *you like me,* he'd said. Like I hadn't been trying for two years to let him know. Like I hadn't been terrified to let him know.

Greg, Ryan, Chad, Lysander.

I wish he'd never gone to California.

"Hey, Lysander." Frank walked over, and I whipped back around in my chair so I wouldn't be caught gazing at him. It would only make things worse. "Ricky said he established this server connection, but I'm not finding it on the—"

I focused on the chicken scratch and tuned them out. Worked it out a bit at a time. Some words were so slanted and tiny I had to deduce what they were from context alone. Busting out a highlighter, I marked up a few lines I never would be able to identify on my own. I'd have to give this guy a personal visit tomorrow and have him read them to me.

Laughter drew me out of my thoughts. Frank's laughter.

"Really? I never would have thought," he said.

"It's not just for kids," Lysander explained, and I knew immediately his tabletop RPGs had come into conversation. "It's fun. You should try sometime. You can do it online with modulators that calculate all the math for you."

Frank shrugged. "We'll see." He vanished back into his cubicle.

I stared after him, then at Lysander, who noticed and quirked an eyebrow. "What?"

My thoughts churned as I came up with the nicest way to put what was on my mind. "You're just . . . you don't seem as shy as you used to be." Ever since he came back to Utah, I'd noticed his confidence building. Little bit by little bit. His stutter was softening. His expression was becoming more open with those he wasn't familiar with.

He looked surprised for a moment, then shrugged it off. "Guess that's another thing I fixed."

I stared at him a moment. He put his hand on his desk like he was going to turn back around, but he didn't. Like he was waiting for me to say something.

So I did. "That's funny."

His dark brows drew together. "What's funny?"

"You talk like you were broken."

He rolled his eyes. But he still didn't turn around.

One of the crushed butterflies twitched its antennae, and I wondered.

Softer, so Frank wouldn't overhear, "Were you?"

He paused. It was subtle, the way he went still. His chest stopped moving, his neck tensed, he didn't blink for a couple beats. He stared at the floor, or rather through the floor to something I couldn't see. After a few seconds, he said, "I don't know. Maybe."

The tiny confession pushed into my chest. He looked so pensive, so tired . . . almost like how he'd looked in the parking lot, before I vomited my feelings and ruined everything. Not that I entirely blamed myself for what happened, but still.

"I don't think you're broken. Then, or now," I whispered, and I turned back to my work, embarrassed that I'd said it, worried it was corny. I tried to focus on chicken scratch, but my mind was too conflicted for that, so I pulled over the document and tried to make sentences out of bullet points.

A few minutes later, I felt a tap on my shoulder, right over where my raven tattoo was. I looked back to see Lysander with a box of weird-looking crackers.

"Want some?" He didn't look at me when he said it. It took me back to when we first met. He hadn't been able to look at me then either.

Another antennae twitched. A wing. "Sure." I pulled out a few crackers—they were mottled purple and green. "Smart carbs?"

His lip twitched up again. "Unfortunately."

* ○ *

LYSANDER

What Blaine had said earlier that week stuck with me, even when the weekend finally rolled around to give me and the team a break. My thoughts lingered back at work as I pulled into my parents' driveway and stepped out of my car. *You talk like you were broken.*

But wasn't I? And wasn't I, still? Ever since I was a kid, I envied others' ability to just speak up, to say what was on their mind without fear of the consequences. To walk up to someone they didn't know and ask them to play. To be able to easily answer a question when the teacher called on them, without shrinking into their desk and second-guessing whether the answer they had was the right answer, or feeling humiliated when it wasn't.

As an adult, I understood more that most of that anxiety was with me, not others. If I said a joke and no one laughed, I felt like a complete moron, but really, no one else noticed or cared as much as I did. I *knew* that, but I couldn't stop rampant thoughts and self-analyzing every time I opened my mouth around someone I wasn't completely comfortable with, and that list was short.

Blaine had been on that list. Sometimes I wish I'd kept my mouth shut in that parking lot, or said something different, so she could have stayed on it. But the past was the past and what I felt was still valid. Even if the other feelings surrounding it sucked.

Yet she'd had a point. I hadn't realized it until she pointed it out. I didn't know Frank well. Only by name, before my promotion. And I'd casually chatted with him about tabletop games after he mentioned his son's interest in them. Once, I'd been embarrassed to share that I liked role-playing, period. Now I was recommending it to colleagues. I'd enjoyed it. And I didn't want to think too hard on the exchange. I didn't want to shrink inside my shell.

However much I hated the awkward social aspects of being, well, more fit than I'd been before, maybe it was helping me. Or maybe all the attention was *forcing* me to become comfortable with it. Just like the new job was forcing me to stretch outside my comfort zone too. And I was glad . . . but I also wasn't sure whether or not I was fixing something that was broken, or simply evolving for the better.

I turned the knob on my parents' front door; unlocked, as expected.

What was not expected was the young woman sitting at the dining table with my mom and dad.

Before I could ask, my mother jumped to her feet and rushed over to me. "Here he is! Lysander, you remember Abigail, from down the street?"

My eyes swept from my mother back to the woman. She . . . looked vaguely familiar. "Uh—"

Abigail. Abby. Abby Anderson. My neighbor. Or, rather, my neighbor's daughter. If my mother hadn't gabbed about her earlier, about her earning her master's degree in psychology, I might not have put two and two together.

And I might not have known exactly why Abby was here.

I pushed down frustration at being bombarded with a *date*, with my *parents*, especially given that my mother knew firsthand that I didn't exactly blossom in these sorts of interactions. But I pasted a smile on my face and said, "Hi."

I left my IO Masters lanyard on, my photo hanging from it.

My mother pulled my laptop bag off my shoulder and set it on the sofa, then pushed me toward the table. "Here, sit, I'll get the casserole." She hurried to the oven.

My father cracked open a can of Mountain Dew and poured it into his glass. He was a three-sodas-a-day kind of person, as his dentist was well aware. "Abby is getting her master's degree in psychology," he said matter-of-factly. Like he may or may not have been coached into pushing the matter when I arrived.

I wanted to nod and fiddle with my silverware, or maybe grab my cup and fill it at the sink. But I forced myself to meet

Abby's eyes—they were pretty, hazel—and say, "So I heard. Must be hard."

"It's really interesting, actually." She leaned to the side as my mother set a casserole in the center of the table. "Thank you, for the invitation."

"Of course!" My mother took a seat at the head of the table and said grace. She only did that when we had company. She served Abby and then herself, then passed the spoon to me. I gave myself a fist-sized helping before my dad scooped a third of the dish onto his plate.

Abby said, "Right now we're studying the psychology of love. It's really fascinating. There was this study done on fatty diets in rabbits, but one group of rabbits was faring much better than the second, despite eating all the same things. When the researchers looked into it, they discovered one of the caregivers was cuddling the rabbits in her charge, while the other didn't. The cuddle-rabbits were the healthier ones."

"Huh." That *was* interesting. "Kind of like those stories with the orphanages." How infants in orphanages developed better when they were held than when they weren't. I'd seen a thing on the news a few years ago.

"Exactly. Or how the Volkswagen Bug was designed to look like a baby's face."

"Was it?" my dad chimed in. He thought for a moment. "I guess it does."

Abby went on, "We're naturally acclimated to be endeared to those proportions. So yeah, it's interesting." She picked at her food. "Your mom says you fix computers?"

"IT, yeah."

"Oh, right. That's a little different." She smiled. "What else do you like to do?"

My mother answered for me, "He likes to go on hikes and volunteer at the animal shelter." She beamed.

I glanced at her. I maybe hiked twice a year and I volunteered at the Humane Society one semester in high school for extra credit.

My thoughts returned to Frank. To being uncomfortable. To loving myself better.

"I actually like role-playing games," I said, and my mother's face blanched.

Abby blinked. "Role-playing games? Like those video games?"

"Sometimes video games, but a lot of them are pretty weak on story," I offered. "I like tabletop better. You know, Pathfinder, Dungeons & Dragons, Call of Cthulhu."

She smiled, though I could tell she was confused. She took a bite of casserole.

"And he loves dogs." My mother kicked me under the table.

That was true. When I moved out of my apartment into a house, I planned to get a dog.

"I've heard of one of those," Abby said, her voice light and pleasant, like she was answering the phone at a call center. "But not . . . cathlu?"

"Cthulhu," I said, and ate a cheesy, breaded piece of broccoli. "It's an ancient deity created by H. P. Lovecraft. Has an octopus for a head."

"Oh." She laughed. It sounded a little forced.

"How are your parents?" my dad asked without looking up from his plate.

"Oh, they're good. They have a trip planned for Italy next spring . . ."

I focused on my meal as they chatted, slipping into my usual, quiet role at the table.

And I really didn't mind.

• • ○

Blaine was already in our shared work cubicle when I stopped by a couple minutes before five the following Wednesday. She'd been staying later than Frank and I the last two days.

She didn't notice me. She was scrolling through a document, one hand on the computer mouse, one on her keyboard, fingers flying across the keys, inputting various keyboard commands. She'd worn a cardigan today, and but now it hung off the back of her chair, revealing the sleeveless pink blouse underneath. Her hair, a hint of blue showing through, lay over smooth shoulders. I could see the edge of the raven's tail, from her tattoo, peeking out from her sleeve.

Like God himself had snapped his fingers, I was in her entryway again, chuckling softly as she made fun of my own tattoo. Afterward, I couldn't believe I'd actually shown her. Only my gaming buddies knew about it, and only Mark had seen it, since he'd been with me when I got it. My parents and brothers didn't know it existed.

What would I have done, if she'd said it then? *I like you.* Before Ashley laughed at my pictures, before people I barely remembered messaged me on social media, before the Hooked messages and the surprise neighbor dinners. What would I have said?

I wouldn't have believed her.

Did I believe her now?

My heartbeat picked up. I tried to think of something to

say . . . I don't know, because I wanted her to notice me. I wanted her to look at me. I wanted things to be the way they were before.

Maybe Blaine *didn't* smile at everyone.

After another few seconds, I settled on, "Passionate for infrastructure, huh?"

She started and spun around. She had a pair of blue-light glasses on and . . .

And . . .

I forgot what I was going to . . . think.

Something about her right then, with the setting sun streaming through the window, with her hair down, with her skin tone contrasted with the pink blouse, and those dark frames highlighting bright blue eyes . . . suddenly I knew what I would have said, had she told me then, in the entryway.

I would have said, *I like you too.*

"Choke on your coffee?" she asked, and I realized I'd been gawking. Retreating a step, I felt my face heat and prayed my skin was tan enough to hide it. My father had once said it was something he envied about me, and I'd clung to that fact since I was a teenager. *The tan hides it. The tan hides it.* It made me a little less of a mess in social situations.

I also realized I was still holding a very hot cup of coffee. I set it down.

She turned back to her screen, making me oddly disappointed that she was more absorbed in work than in me . . . and I felt like a tool for even thinking it. I was the one who'd turned her down in the parking lot. Maybe if I hadn't been so tired . . . if I hadn't still been riled up with the executive assistant's comments, I would have said something else. I should have said something else.

"Game tonight," she said, and the scrolling, clicking, and typing resumed. "I'm not missing this one."

That explained the early start and the late nights. I nodded, not that she could see it. Frank swung by to check in, then I sat at my desk. Went through the motions of pulling up my files and opening applicable software, but I was distracted. And the more I thought about it, the more frustrating the distraction came.

I'd always liked Blaine. She'd been friendly to me from the start. But maybe that was the problem. She had those superpowers I'd envied all my life. The power to chat up literally anyone who passed by. The power to shrug off mistakes like a light jacket. The power to stand her ground when she was right about something.

I hadn't really dated anyone since college. That was, before Ashley. I hadn't exactly been most girls' first pick. The shy, overweight loner in the corner who could barely string a sentence together . . . and before dating apps, I didn't know where to meet girls, anyway. So when a pretty new hire came in and smiled at me, and complimented my taste in superheroes . . . and then smiled and laughed with everyone else in the building, I knew it was just that superpower. I knew it wasn't anything more.

I like you, she'd said.

And that made me angry.

I pushed my headphones over my ears and turned on a random alternative station. After about a quarter hour, I was able to focus on work. At this rate, we'd have everything ready for beta testing next month, which was within the deadline the CEO wanted. It would be my first success as a product manager. Proof that I could do new, bigger, and better things.

At six o'clock, a flash of black caught the corner of my eye. I turned to see Blaine pulling on her cardigan, then pack up her laptop. I pulled my headphones down. "You're leaving already?"

"I've put in forty-one hours this week already, and it's only hump day." She stated it so directly, and with one raised eyebrow, like she was daring me to challenge her. "The draft user guide is ready and the staff presentation is outlined. Can't do any more on that until this guy gets me his notes." She jutted her finger toward Frank. "So yes. See you tomorrow."

She waved, then hurried down the aisle. Judging by her footsteps, she took off at a run once she reached the main hall.

I sighed. Fair was fair—she *had* been pulling an awful lot of overtime. We all had, since we couldn't spare more labor for Infrared without hurting other ongoing projects. The developers were already overloaded. Turning back to my computer, I pulled up some code and glanced over it before my eyes fell to an icon pinned to my taskbar.

IO Chat. The company instant messenger.

Curious, maybe bored, I clicked on it. The last message was from three and a half weeks ago. From Blaine. No one else had messaged me since. A conversation about cats.

I felt angry all over again. Rubbed at a sucking sensation between my lungs. Closed out the box and got back to work.

A few minutes later, I got an email from the vice president, with attached images for Infrared's customer-facing wall. I downloaded them and went to save them on the thumb drive.

The computer couldn't find it.

I glanced at my empty USB ports. Tapped my fingers for half a second before remembering I'd given it to Blaine last night so she could adequately describe enrollment in the user guide. I swiveled around.

Blaine's desk was empty except for a few papers.

Cursing under my breath, I pulled off my headphones entirely and went over, shuffling the documents around, searching for a thumb drive . . . but it wasn't there. It was probably still plugged into her laptop.

Which she'd taken with her.

I pulled my phone from my pocket, ignoring new notifications, and swiped to her contact information. Pushed Call.

She answered right before I would be sent to voicemail.

"What."

The noise in the background told me she was driving. "You have the thumb drive I need."

She cursed. "I can't turn around. I'll bring it to you first thing in the morning."

"I need it now." I couldn't do anything else today without that thumb drive, and I didn't want to work insanely late on Friday too. I . . . had a Hooked date I wasn't incredibly enthused to attend.

"Then I'll bring it later tonight if you want to camp out." I heard the clicking of a turn signal. "If I go back now, I'll miss my game. Take a break, Lysander. We're ahead of schedule."

"We're *on* schedule—"

"Then come get it." Her tone grew sharp. "Because I am not missing another game."

Sighing, I pinched the bridge of my nose. "Where are you?"

"I'm at the Malone Training Center."

That wasn't too far. "Fine," I said, and hung up. Rubbed

my eyes. I still needed to eat dinner—I had turkey meatballs, mashed potatoes, and sugar snap peas awaiting me in the fridge. But this trip shouldn't take long. I'd grab it when I got back.

Leaning over my computer, I saved a few files, finished reviewing another, then shut my laptop and grabbed my keys. "Be back," was all I said to Frank.

○ ● ●

My phone buzzed when I neared the training center. After I parked, I checked the text.

> **Blaine:** It's in my duffel bag behind the bleachers.
> Black bag with green straps.

Shoving the phone in my pocket, I crossed the nearly full lot to the front doors. A cheer went out from within. Inside, there was a small vendor station with prepackaged food for sale, then a table set up for ticket sales. The gal behind it looked up from her phone when I approached. I saw her eyes glance at my wrist, probably searching for an entry band.

"Tickets are ten for adults," she said.

I shrunk inwardly. "I, uh . . . I'm just here to pick up a thing. A thumb drive. From Blaine. Wickers?"

"Oh, yeah." She jutted her thumb over her shoulder. "She mentioned it."

I waved my thanks and continued into the hall behind her, pausing once, wondering if I should ask for directions. I'd never been one for sports, and I'd never been inside this facility before, so I felt very outside my element. After a couple seconds of standing in the hallway, I decided to keep going, hoping there weren't too many sets of bleachers, or I wouldn't be back nearly as quickly as I thought.

Passing a bathroom, I turned the corner and came across a few more vendor tables of random things—clothing, salsa, hair accessories. Just beyond them I spied a triangular cluster of bleachers. Beyond those was a large gym floor with a giant oval taped down on it. One mass of women churned on one end of the oval while another skater with a star on her helmet zipped around the track. They wore tank tops or T-shirts, ripped fishnets, bedazzled leg warmers, very short shorts—

I turned my attention to the bleachers and squeezed past a few people who had set up lawn chairs for a better view, which was probably against fire code, but . . . shrugging to myself, I slipped behind the bleachers, finding several bags and water bottles stashed there. Fortunately, Blaine's was right in front. The thumb drive was tucked in the side pocket—her laptop was probably in her car, unless they had lockers here.

Pocketing the drive, I turned to head back, but another cheer went up, and I paused and looked back to the track. I didn't know exactly how roller derby worked, but it sounded kind of like football, if football was on a circuit and all the players were on wheels. The cluster of women had moved, and now the one with the star on her helmet was dancing on her brakes, trying to push through.

"Excuse me," I said to one of the lawn-chairers, whose legs were blocking the way. He moved them without a second glance my direction. *Just curious,* I thought. I wouldn't stay too long without paying for a ticket. That, and I had work to do back at the—

At the—

The cluster had broken apart; the shrill notes of a referee's whistle still permeated the air. I noticed Blaine almost immediately; her brown-and-blue hair was braided over her shoulder, and her name was in rhinestones on the back of a very fitted tank top: *Blaine Witch Project.*

She turned the corner with a few other players, and my entire torso warmed. She had eye black on her cheekbones, more rhinestones across her chest, and very short sequined shorts on her long legs—

Very . . . *nice* . . . looking legs.

She swept right by, focused on the game and oblivious to me.

And I just stood there, gaping at flexing quads and hamstrings.

She could kill me with the back of her knee. Literally pop my head right off my neck.

A couple players skated off the rink. I shook myself and backed away, checking my pocket three times for the thumb drive before I reached the vendors, feeling a little warmer with each step.

Crossing the parking lot, driving the car, and sitting at my desk, I couldn't stop seeing *Blaine Witch Project* on the back of my eyelids.

I didn't get much done, and went home at 7:35.

Chapter 11

BLAINE

I WAS WAITING on my panini press when Rue thumped up the stairs on the house, knocking twice on the door at the top before letting herself in. I did a double take—her usually messy, faded hair was freshly dyed pink and straightened, she wore makeup, and a *skirt*.

She saw my eyes and said, "It has pockets."

I remembered her mentioning she had a date tonight. Another Hooked pairing. "Curfew is eleven."

She rolled her eyes and helped herself to my fridge.

"Aren't you going out to eat?"

"Yeah, but I'm hungry now." Selecting a string cheese, she closed the fridge with her foot and opened the package, eating it one chunk at a time instead of peeling it. A more sanitary way to consume string cheese, for sure, but it still felt wrong to me.

She glanced at my sweats and steaming panini press. "Staying in again." It wasn't a question.

I shrugged. "I found some Tudor historical on Netflix I thought I'd binge."

I felt her eyes on me as my press beeped and I plucked out my sandwich with a fork. After a few seconds, she asked, "Want to come to Herospect with me tomorrow?"

I snorted. "No, thank you. I'm fresh out of foam swords."

"You can NPC. Be an extra. Earn points if you ever want to be a main."

It was nice of her to offer, but I shook my head. LARPing just wasn't my thing. "Nah. I'm going to apply for some more jobs and do some online shopping."

She leaned against the counter. It was 6:45; I had a feeling she needed to leave. "You've been kind of out of it since . . . the thing."

The thing is what she called the disaster with Lysander. I sighed. "I know. I'm just tired from all the overtime."

"I bet."

"It should end soon, though." I really wanted it to end. I wanted my evenings back.

A stupid part of me didn't want it to.

Another long pause passed before Rue said, "He's not worth your time."

My chest felt hollow; I took a bite of turkey and cranberry on wheat to fill it. "I know." But things were starting to feel normalish again between us, and it made it hard to be angry at him. We still weren't instant messaging in the middle of the day or taking lunch together, but . . . I guess I was just a stupid kicked dog who crawled back to its owner.

I still wanted him. So badly. I loved the sound of his voice and his laugh. I knew he'd watch the Tudor series with me and comment on the historically inappropriate costumes. I missed hearing about the latest plot turn in his gaming. I wanted him to come to derby games and cheer me on. I wanted *anyone* to come to derby games and cheer me on. Because all my friends were on the track and all my family lived elsewhere.

Standing there with a half-chewed bite of panini in my mouth, I suddenly felt like I was going to cry. Like that little hollow space in my chest had black-holed and was going to consume all of me.

I just wanted to go home.

Rue touched my shoulder. "I can stay here."

Shaking myself, I swallowed and smiled. "I'm okay. Have fun."

Maybe I should move back home. There was a lot in Utah that I loved—Rue, namely. The Salt Lake Sinners. The job opportunities. The mountains and forests. Lysander.

But my résumés were already out, and doing well. Maybe that was a sign.

Rue squeezed my shoulder and headed out the front door. I stood by the counter, eating my panini, thinking about my murky future. Even if I went back to Washington, I probably wouldn't get a job super close to my mom. The Palouse didn't even have a gas station. The closest I'd likely get was in Spokane, which was nearly a two-hour drive away. But at least I'd have the option to drive out on the weekends and go to lunch with my mom or something. I could get in touch with some high school friends too.

The rest, I'd have to start from scratch, just like I did here.

Which of course made me think of horrible confession number two, which completely wiped out my sphere of friends and made me start from the bottom up all over again. But hey, that meant I'd had a lot of practice, right?

As I shoved the last bit of sandwich into my mouth, my phone chimed. Email. I clicked on it and stood straighter. Another request for a phone interview for another tech company.

In Spokane.

Maybe it's a sign.

Wiping my hands on my shirt, I hurried to my room, where my computer was, so I could respond right away. Someone was apparently working on the weekends for me to get that email now, but I wanted to show I was responsive and on top of things, and I hated writing out emails on a phone. I'd reply now.

Maybe things were looking up. Maybe this was a good thing.

I could only hope it was.

* ○ *

Not fair.

I sat in that stupid cubicle on the stupid third floor of stupid IO Masters, thumbs dancing over my phone screen. Pain shot up my jaw from clenching my teeth so hard as I typed out the response.

Me: I don't think I'm going to make it. I'm so sorry.

If I wasn't so mad, or maybe so used to disappointment by now, I might have cried. But we had a hard Friday deadline for this next round on Infrared, and it was Wednesday, and I didn't even remember what life was like before overtime.

Maybe it's for the best, I thought as I shoved my phone

between my knees and forced my jaw to relax. *If I go to Washington, I'll have to leave the Salt Lake Sinners, anyway.*

Because I'd had my phone interview that morning, this time in my car, with my lunch sitting uneaten next to me because my stomach was full of nerves. And the interview had gone really well. The company was called Ruthford, and it did integrated solutions for public safety—like the software 911 dispatchers, cops, and firefighters used. It was something I could really get behind, something that would make me feel like I was helping the world. Solid-state storage devices didn't really tickle my knickers.

I had a second phone interview scheduled for *Monday.* And yes, the job would come with a pay raise. And wheat-covered hills and farmers markets and hayrides and my mom. No more Carol, no more Utah winter smog . . . no more derby, no more Lysander.

I glanced back at him. He had a piece of hardware I didn't recognize out on his desk that he was messing with and occasionally turned to type something into his computer. Something I'd probably end up translating into lay terms later.

My phone buzzed. I checked the screen.

> **Rue:** Well that's great because Yolanda just sprained her ankle in warm-ups.

A curse tumbled out of my mouth. Yolanda was another blocker. If I wasn't there, and Yolanda was out, we wouldn't have enough people to play, unless—

> **Rue:** So I'm getting ready for some bruises.

I sighed. Rue would have to block when she wasn't up for jamming, and the rest we'd have to wing. Maybe one of our retirees could come in . . .

"What's wrong?"

I started, then swiveled in my chair toward Lysander, whose stupid handsome face and newly trimmed beard was looking at me with one stupid dark eyebrow raised. As per usual, I didn't hold back. "I'm missing another derby game tonight, and one of our other blockers is injured. So we'll have to finagle something or forfeit."

I hated forfeiting. It was the worst way to lose, and the worst way to win.

"Oh," he said, thumb playing with that hardware. "I'm sorry."

"Hmm," was all I said. I supposed this time it wasn't Lysander's fault, just IO Masters's. Them and their ridiculous deadlines that didn't take into account that people had lives outside of work. Frank had a wife and kids, and he was often here later than I was.

I turned back to my monitor. "I'm about five seconds from just quitting and heading over there."

"Don't quit."

Something about that rankled me. "Don't have much reason to stay right now."

I glanced at the shortcut to the company instant messenger, and in my mind's eye some stupid GIF popped up in it, something that would make me laugh and feel a little better. Something that would take the edge off.

It'd been a month since someone sent me a GIF.

"It will get better," he offered. "Infrared isn't forever."

"Maybe." I opened up a file. "But we both know Carol is as eternal as Satan."

He chuckled softly. The sound hurt. It hurt like a spike right between my breasts, pushing slowly through skin, muscle, and bone. It hurt because I loved that sound and I didn't get to hear it much anymore, especially not directed to me. It hurt because I wished so badly that *he* was the reason I had to stay.

Without really thinking of it, I mumbled, "I miss who you were." Then heard the words in my ears and felt dumb, so I fake-focused on the document in front of me. Which I really should get done, since the Sinners were losing a game for this.

Several beats passed before Lysander, equally quiet, said, "Then why didn't you like *him*?"

I jerked around, chair squeaking, that chest pain flashing down into my gut. He didn't meet my eyes at first, distracted by that hardware. I waited until those dark orbs met mine.

There was not a gram of joking in my tone when I said, "The fact that you just asked me that question shows how utterly ignorant you are."

His brows shot up. I'd surprised him. Good.

My phone buzzed. I turned back to my screen and pulled it out. Not super subtly, since Lysander also used his phone for sanity during overtime and was hardly going to tell me to put it away. I expected something from Rue, an official word of forfeit or the like, but to my surprise, the text was from Nora.

Nora: Hey, are you still around?

Confused, I typed back.

Me: Yeah . . . are you?

Nora: Yeah. I've been pulling overtime this week to get this presentation done before I leave. And, well, I think I've cut it a little too close.

Me: Uh, yeah you are. Wasn't your due date two days ago?

Nora: My water just broke . . .

I gasped.

Me: ARE YOU SERIOUS???

"What's wrong?" Lysander asked.
But my thumbs were flying.

Me: Go to the hospital!

Nora: Oh, I would love to. But I take Frontrunner to work, remember? And there's a nasty accident in Salt Lake and my husband can't get here . . . I'm really sorry, but can you give me a ride?

"Blaine?" Lysander asked as I hit the Call button on my phone. It rang once before Nora answered.
"Are you okay?" I asked the moment it clicked.

The first response was a muffled grunt. "Oh, yeah. As okay as I can be. It's, uh, happening kind of fast."

"I'm coming. I'm coming. Hold on." I jumped from my chair and grabbed my bag, not bothering to pack my laptop.

Lysander stood as well. "What's wrong?"

Frank glanced over.

"Nora's water broke. She needs a ride to the hospital." I paused. "I'm sorry. I'll hit the deadline—"

He shook his head. "No, it's okay. Go."

I nodded my thanks and bolted down the aisles to the stairs, taking them two at a time to the fourth floor. I found Nora in her cubicle, still on her chair, bent over with her hands clamped on her knees. She breathed deeply. Her chair and part of the floor were wet.

I'd never had a baby, but I'm pretty sure when the water broke, that meant go time.

"Can you walk?" I asked, grasping her shoulder, ready to carry her on my back if I needed to.

She glanced up at me. Her left eye twitched like she was in pain and doing a good job of hiding it. "Yes, I can walk." She stood slowly. I kept my grip on her arm and slowly led her toward the elevator.

"You shouldn't be here!" I snatched her purse off the desk as we passed it.

"I know. I know." She took a deep breath through her mouth and out her nose. "We're just so shorthanded, and Carol was so adamant about it—"

"Carol can suck a lemon." I glanced down at her wet legs when we reached the elevator and I smacked the down button. "Do you have a change of clothes?"

She laughed. "No. And it won't matter; they'll put me in a"—she hissed at a contraction—"gown once I get there anyway."

"Okay. Okay. It's okay. I will speed like the devil." My heart was racing and my palms were clammy, but I kept a grip on Nora and focused on the task at hand. Eased her into the elevator and pushed the button for the main floor. We were silent as the elevator slowly lowered. The receptionist had already gone home. As we crossed the lobby, I noticed Nora's right shoe squeaked. Probably because it had gotten wet.

"I'll send flowers to the janitor," I offered.

Nora laughed. "Probably a good idea." Then she winced again.

I pushed her a little faster. Weren't these contractions pretty close together? What was the rule for contractions? I checked my watch, ready to start timing them, but when we reached the front doors, something dawned on me, and I cursed loud enough for it to echo all the way back to the elevators.

"What?" Nora asked.

I let out a long breath. "I took my bike."

"What?"

"My motorcycle," I ground out, cursing that decision. "I drove my motorcycle to work."

Nora's face fell. "Well, we'll make it work. It will be funny . . . later."

Yeah, hilarious. A woman about to burst with child, having regular contractions, holding on to me for dear life on a motorcycle as we sped our way to the hospital.

"At least we can weave if there's traffic," I offered, turning and pushing the door open with my shoulder. "I'm so sorry."

"It's okay."

"I can drive."

We both froze between the storm doors in the breezeway as Lysander approached—I hadn't even heard him. He didn't have his laptop case either—he hadn't been planning to go home. Must have come out to check on us.

Relief slid, cool and blissful, down my throat. "Really? Are you sure?"

"He's sure," Nora pressed, and waddled for the last set of doors.

Meeting Lysander's eyes, I mouthed, *Thank you.*

He nodded and pulled out his keys.

Chapter 12

I'D READIED MYSELF for a fight on the way to the American Fork Hospital while sitting in the back seat of Lysander's Camry, pressed up against the back of the passenger seat and holding Nora's hand. Woman had a *grip*. I asked her about her other kids and what they were doing in school, and when she stopped answering, I started blathering about anything and everything I could think of. Roller derby, politics, my mom, even Infrared. I knew that if I was anxious and in pain, I'd want someone distracting me. I think it helped, but it was hard to tell.

Lysander's knuckles were white on the steering wheel as he weaved through traffic, never saying a word. He zipped through the hospital parking lot when we arrived and pulled up right to the doors of the building with the maternity ward. Bolting out of the car, I helped Nora from her seat and inside. Her waddle was worse. Her pants were newly wet, like she'd leaked more. I'd pay to have Lysander's car cleaned later.

Fortunately, the fight I was amped up to have never happened. Hospital workers took one look at Nora and rushed to get her a wheelchair. I stayed right by her side, assuring her even as she assured me that she'd had babies before. I crammed into the back of the elevator and saw her all the way to the maternity ward doors, which locked from the inside.

I'd met Nora's husband a few times at company parties and searched the rest of the floor for him, but to no avail. Took the stairs down and scanned the main lobby, then the parking lot. Lysander was nowhere in sight, but we did have a Friday deadline. I'd have to Uber back to work or something . . . but I couldn't just leave Nora here. Not until her baby daddy arrived.

Hands cold, I took the elevator back up to the maternity ward and paused when the doors opened to the lobby. Lysander was there, sitting on a floral bench, elbows on his knees. He glanced up when I approached.

"I thought you left." I sat across from him, then stood again, too nervous to hold still. So I paced.

"And strand you two here?" He shook his head.

Pace, pace, pace. "Nora's going to be in for a while. I know we have a deadline, but—"

"Don't worry about it." He rubbed his eyes. "We'll make it work. And if it's late, they can deal."

Gratitude pricked my skin. "Thank you." I paused pacing and wrung my hands together. "I just don't want to leave until her husband gets here."

He nodded.

A few seconds of silence passed between us. A receptionist came out to the desk, glanced at us, then focused on her computer.

"You can go home," I offered. "You don't have to stay."

His dark eyes glanced up at me. "And how will you get home?"

"Uber," I offered. "Rue. Bus."

He simply shook his head again. "I'll wait. Besides, I like Nora."

I smiled at that, then glanced at the doors. "Okay, I'm going to see if they'll let me in. Her husband's name is Clint. Big balding guy, mustache."

Lysander looked so tired again, but his lip curved into a half smile. "I'll look out for him."

Nodding my thanks, I went to the receptionist. "Excuse me, my friend Nora Patterson just checked in. Her water broke, but her family isn't here yet. Is there any way—"

"Are you Blaine?" she asked.

I nodded.

Grabbing a clipboard, she came around the desk. "I just put you on the visitor list on her request. Come on."

Relief sighed right out of me as I followed her to the secured double doors. Lysander glanced over, and I gave him two thumbs up as the receptionist buzzed me in and took me to Nora's room.

Nora was already in a gown and lying on a bed; a nurse had just finished putting in an IV for her. When she saw me, her first question was, "Clint?"

"Not yet." I hurried to her side. "If you give me his number, I can call him."

"I can still operate a phone." She laughed, then grunted. Lines on a monitor next to her spiked with the contraction. When it ended, she said, "If he's not here when this baby comes, I'm going to rip that mustache off."

"I'm sure he's trying really hard." I rubbed Nora's arm, the one that didn't have an IV in it.

She rested back on the pillows. The nurse came over with a cup of ice chips. "The anesthesiologist will be here soon . . . but we might pass the window for an epidural by then."

Nora swore, and I gaped. I'd never heard a foul word exit her mouth before. Then again, epidurals seemed like something worth swearing over.

The nurse left. Another, smaller contraction rippled on the monitor. Nora breathed deeply through it. I gave her my other hand to squeeze, since the knuckles on the other still hurt from her grip in the car. It passed, and she relaxed.

"Why have you been so down lately?" She shook a couple ice chunks into her mouth.

"Me?" I asked. "You're in labor and we're going to talk about *me?*"

Ice crunched between her teeth. "Distract me. Either talk or start a song and dance."

"Um." I glanced at the door, but even the nurse had left, and Lysander had not managed to get through the security doors and wander into the room. So.

"You two have a fight?" she guessed, then breathed deep as another contraction hit. I set my jaw as she squeezed the life out of my fingers, but didn't dare complain. I'd much rather lose feeling in my hand then push a baby out of my hoo-ha.

"What? No. I mean, it's just Lysander—"

"Until I have an epidural"—she looked straight into my eyes—"there will be no bullcrap in this room. I don't have patience for bullcrap, Blaine."

Yeesh. Nora was not her usual nice, chipper self when she was extricating babies.

I exhaled and let my lips vibrate with it.

"If it helps, I already know." She chewed up another ice chip. "It's obvious, so spill."

My stomach flipped. "You do? I mean—"

She shot me a hard look.

I fidgeted, but Nora's death grip kept me from fleeing. "Obvious to everyone but him, maybe."

"Men are dense." She squeezed my hand with a contraction, and I bit the meat of my thumb when she did. Good heavens, she could crack walnuts with that grip!

"Maybe," I offered, once she relaxed again. "I . . . told him. That I liked him. He didn't take it well."

"Really?" she looked genuinely surprised. "I don't believe that."

I frowned. "Believe it or not." But her shock stuck with me. She said it was so obvious . . . did she think it was obvious on Lysander's end too?

Suddenly I remembered our exchange in that cubicle, right before Nora texted me and everything flew out of my brain. *Then why didn't you like* him? he'd asked. And I was so taken aback by the question, so confused, that I'd called him ignorant.

Because I *had* liked "him." I liked all of Lysander, past and present. And I had for *two years*.

What was I missing?

"Maybe something's going on with him," Nora offered, rattling the ice in her cup. "He's had a lot of changes lately."

I glanced at the door. "Yeah, maybe." I spun through the exchange again, then all the ones before that. The parking lot, the IMs . . . I barely noticed when Nora squeezed the life out of my hand again.

"You would know better than me." Her voice was tense as the contraction ebbed.

I should. But I didn't.

Shallow, he'd said. Why would he call me shallow?

Why did he break up with Ashley?

My stomach sank a little. Did he think I only liked him for his looks now? But there was *no way.* Like Nora confirmed—I'd been so obvious. I'd drowned him in invitations and hints. He'd never taken me up on them. He was so shy, but like Rue had said, what more could I have done? Jumped in his lap? Tied him up in my bra and panties and made out with him?

I'd *told* him. I'd finally *told* him, and . . . and . . .

I let out a long breath, like *I* was the one contracting. Was there a hurt in Lysander I was just oblivious to? Or was that just another pointless, hopeful thought? My brain trying to make it work when it already so blatantly hadn't?

"I don't know," I whispered.

The door bursting open scared me enough that I ripped my hand from Nora's vise grip. I nearly melted at the side of Clint, his hair mussed and suit jacket askew.

"Oh thank God," Nora said, emotion leaking into her voice.

I stepped back as Clint approached and took Nora's hand in his. "I'm so sorry. I'm so sorry. There was a rollover—"

I slipped into the hallway to give them some privacy. Escorted myself down the hall and back through the security doors to the lobby. Lysander was still there, though now he was standing, one hand in his pocket, one holding his phone.

The sight of him sent a thrill through me, both pleasant and unpleasant. Sort of like riding a rollercoaster downhill.

I like you, I'd said, but I'd been wrong. I really did *love* Lysander May. Even though he called me shallow, even though we didn't instant message anymore . . . I wanted nothing more than to cross the room and put my arms around his waist—big or small—and rest my head between his shoulder blades. Breathe in his scent, slip my hand into his, and say, *Let's go home.*

I flexed the hand Nora had mangled. I'd push a baby out of my nethers for Lysander May.

And that realization, that *want,* hurt. Hurt more than heartburn and derby bruises and maybe more than contractions, but I didn't have any firsthand experiences with those. But it hurt in a draining, empty, exhausting way that threatened tears. I swallowed and took a deep breath. I'd get over it eventually, right? I had to.

I missed him. So much.

Steeling myself, pasting on a smile, I crossed the room. Kept my distance. "Thanks for waiting," I said, and braced myself for the impact of his gaze. It was still tired, but it was soft, and in it I saw the old Lysander, the pre–parking lot Lysander, and I had to look away or lose myself in it and confess all over again. The last thing I wanted was to turn four killer rejections into five. "We can head back to work."

And we did.

And that was that.

●　●　○

I pulled up a fresh case study on my computer the next morning, wincing at the wide margins the guy in marketing had put on it. Did he do that on purpose, or had his word processor defaulted to some bizarre setting? And he'd typed it up in a *san serif* font too. Didn't everyone know that bulk text should always be serif? No? Just me?

It was weird, going back to "normal" the morning after taking Nora to the hospital. Things felt like they should be different. Like everyone should be asking about the baby, who was born only an hour after Lysander and I left. Or that today was some sort of random holiday no one celebrated and everyone took off. Or at least a *Friday*. The atmosphere reeked with Friday, but it was only Thursday, and it felt wrong.

I glanced to my instant messenger. I hadn't gone back to my shared Infrared cubicle with Lysander after returning. I'd been so distracted on the ride back, and he'd noticed. *Take it off,* he'd said. *You type fast. We'll get it done tomorrow.*

So I had. And despite all the time that had passed since our last digital conversation, I expected that instant messaging box to pop up on my screen. With . . . I don't know, a GIF of a stork, or an inquiry about how Nora was faring or how I was doing . . . how maybe, after braving the hospital together, we should talk. Or something.

I clicked the shortcut open. Last chat was with NPatterson. Before that, LMay. Something about cats. My cursor hovered over it.

What could I say to him? It seemed that maybe, *maybe*, the pieces for a bridge were there, and one of us just had to build it. And even if Lysander never saw me in a romantic light, I wanted his friendship. I missed him, even if I could never *have* him.

Maybe if I just started with *Hey.*

I nearly missed Carol's too subtle start of our morning meeting. Had I not heard papers shuffling at seven o'clock, I would have. My cursor flew up to the X on the instant messenger and I pushed off from my desk, smoothing my slacks as I stood. Grabbed the closest pad of paper, which happened to be a stack of sticky notes, and a pen.

I glanced to the filing cabinet, aka the tombstone for the wheat-and-resin pen Lysander had given me for my birthday. It really was a nice pen . . . it would be a shame to let it go to waste.

Kristi approached. I forced myself to follow after. Morning meetings were never long. I could go back to poorly formatted case studies and instant messenger politics in a moment.

Carol glanced over her stack of papers with a frown pulling at her mouth. "The sales team has a new presentation they want to use to present to customers in the UK. Kristi, I'm going to send it to you. They want it back ASAP."

"Uh," Kristi began, and Carol's sharp eyes lifted to her. "I can, but do you want me to postpone the *Beehive Monthly* submission?"

Carol's eyes slowly, so slowly, turned back in her head, covered by flickering eyelids as she stifled a groan. *Beehive Monthly* was a state magazine that IO Masters had gotten a spread in—it was good for new recruits and boasted their amazing employee benefits, which were not as amazing in practice as they were on paper.

"No, *Beehives Monthly* first. Blaine, is Infrared finished?"

I choked on a snort. Carol was not amused, and I quickly cleared my expression. "No. I think maybe by Christmas." It wasn't an exaggeration, and I literally had zero more overtime hours to give. Even Carol had to admit that.

Craning, Carol glanced toward Nora's empty desk. "Nora's maternity leave starts today, so she's useless," she griped.

Excuse me?

"Oh!" Kristi lit up. "She had her baby?"

Carol didn't answer, only flipped through papers, so I said, "Yeah, last night at 7:04. Nine-pound boy."

Kristi's eyes bugged. "Big boy."

"Big problem," Carol interjected. "She didn't finish her Pacific conference presentations before she left, and now we have the salesforce biting at our heels. Honestly, we have a schedule for a reason—"

A bad taste crept from the back of my tongue to the front. "We've been aware of her due date since April. She was already pushing it trying to get things done." Carol didn't have kids, and the fact was obvious, but I said it anyway. "You can't plan babies."

"I forgot induction wasn't a thing," she mumbled.

The comment was like an iron bar ramming between my shoulders. "An induction would only have made the baby come *earlier.*"

"Now I have to do this." Carol flung the hand with the papers up. "I have to finish Pacific conference and the salesforce stuff." She glanced back at Nora's desk. "She has her laptop. I'll send her an email—"

Incredulous, I spat, "Are you going to try to get her to *work from the hospital?*"

That sharp glare refocused on me. Kristi backed away.

"I don't like your tone." She waved a hand at both of us. "Get to work. We have no time to dally."

She started to retreat, but I followed her. "If you contact Nora's cell phone or her personal email, I'll report you to HR."

Pausing, Carol glanced back at me. "We're understaffed, Blaine. The company depends on us."

"The company is not upheld on the pillars of four technical writers," I countered, blood running hot.

She pulled her cell phone out of her pocket. "Sit down and get to work."

"Make that three pillars," I said as Carol opened up her contacts and began scrolling. "Because I'm putting in my two weeks' notice. Right now."

Carol's thumb froze over her screen. That's all I saw, because I whirled around and marched back to my desk. Sat down hard enough to make my chair squeak. Snatched my rainbow-lights mouse that Nora had given me.

Nora should quit too. This company was a joke.

And I was done.

○ ● ●

"Blaine Wickers?"

I glanced up from the printout I had of the case study I'd spent my morning formatting and copy editing. A blond guy from HR was standing by my cubicle expectantly.

I checked my monitor—2:37 p.m. "Yeah?"

"Could you come with me?"

Curious, I stood and stuck my phone in my back pocket and followed the guy to the elevators, down to the first floor where HR was. He didn't chat. I didn't try to chat, despite my dislike for awkward silence.

And it was awkward.

He led me right to his glass-walled office and gestured to a seat. Sat down and hit his space bar a couple times to wake up his computer. I never did that—couldn't risk inserting extra spaces into a document and not catching it. I was a mouse-shaker type of gal.

When he didn't talk, I cut to the chase. "Is this about my two weeks' notice?" I'd sent an email this morning about it, since I didn't trust Carol to do it for me.

He nodded. "We're actually going to escort you out today."

I had to think through that statement twice to understand it. "What? But two weeks' notice—"

"You'll be paid for the two weeks," he said, and gave me enough time to mentally fist-pump free money before he said, "but we've identified you as a liability to the company, so your last day will be today."

Fist-pumping slowed. "I'm a liability to the company."

He turned from his computer and pulled a paper from the printer behind his desk. Clicked a pen.

Reading from the paper, he asked, "What prompted you to discontinue your employment at one of Utah's leading technical companies?"

Is it? I eyed him. I was a writer by profession—I knew *persuasive* context when I heard it. The way the question was worded—to uplift the company and put me down—rankled.

But hey, I was about to be unemployed anyway, so . . . honesty time.

"Because the work environment is stifling, the amount of overtime expected ridiculous, and my supervisor is only a supervisor because of longevity, not because she has any managerial expertise or talent whatsoever. She's passive-aggressive and demeaning to her employees."

The guy didn't look up. I glanced at his name plate as

he wrote. *Chad*. Ugh. I hated the name Chad. That video on YouTube made me *loathe* the name Chad.

He did not write long enough to record everything I said, but there was just enough space between us that I couldn't make out the drying ink on the paper. "Do you feel your manager gave you what you needed to succeed?"

I stared at him until he, after several seconds, met my eyes. I'd literally just answered that question, but chose to go with the more polite, "See answer to question one."

He scribbled something down. Made me feel like I was in a doctor's office and a nurse was jotting something like *difficult to work with* in my chart.

"What did you like the best and least about your job."

"The actual work," I answered immediately, just as a blip of Lysander's face echoed in my thoughts. *Escorted out*, they'd said. Guess I wasn't going to say goodbye. Maybe that was for the best, but on the inside I crinkled like a grape in the sun. "I enjoy editing and formatting. For the rest . . . see answer to question one."

They went on like that, pointless question after pointless question. Standard exit interview, though I had a strong suspicion that everything this guy recorded was altered to make me look like some sort of crook. I felt it in my bones. We'd just finished the last question when a soft knock sounded at the office.

I turned around to see Kristi standing there with a box. A box of my stuff. Good heavens, they weren't going to let me clean out my own desk?

"Here," she sounded apologetic as she came in, like she knew she'd been forced to breach office privacy. She set the box on the chair next to me. "Is there anything I missed?"

Withholding comment—this wasn't Kristi's doing—I searched through the box. My lunch bag, my mouse, a couple mugs and pictures were all in there. I sifted through twice before saying, "There's a pen in the bottom drawer of the filing cabinet. A resin pen with wheat in it." I turned toward Chad. "I can just go get it."

"Your colleague can take care of it."

I didn't hide rolling my eyes as Kristi made the trek back to the third floor. Then I turned toward Chad, folded my arms, and glared at him, channeling all the Blaine Witch Project energy I could muster.

After a moment, he turned toward his computer to work, trying to ignore me. But I knew he felt it.

Kristi returned, carrying the pen. I stood, accepted it, and thanked her. I'd never been very close to Kristi, but she was always nice. Did good work. We shook hands and said farewell, and I apologized for the overtime she'd no doubt be pulling now that I was leaving.

Hopefully Carol would be assigned to Infrared in my stead.

Infrared. Lysander. I watched Kristi leave, wondering . . . but there was no way Chad would let me say farewell to anyone when he wouldn't let me retrieve my own pen. Because I was a "liability" to the company.

IO Masters could shove it past their pants seam.

Still, I pulled out my phone, woke the screen . . . and paused. I should text him, right? Just a *Hey, I quit, and they're escorting me out. Sorry about Infrared.* Or something like that. A heads-up. An apology . . . because this was screwing Lysander over too.

I opened my contacts. Scrolled to his name.

Chad stood from his desk, startling me. Oh, go time, I guess. I shoved my phone back in my pocket. He waited by the door—did *not* offer to help me with my things—and literally escorted me all the way to the parking lot. Past the receptionist, lobby, and both storm doors.

Good thing I'd driven my car today.

He didn't say goodbye or wish me luck in my future adventures, he just silently turned back into the building that apparently owned his spine. Whatever. *Two weeks free pay*, I told myself as I walked out to my car. *Two weeks vacation, pretty much.* Which kind of doubly screwed over the writing department, but I was a *liability*, and it literally was not my problem anymore.

At 2:37, I'd walked down to HR.

By 3:14, I was unemployed.

Chapter 13

LYSANDER

I CHECKED MY messenger for the umpteenth time that day. I shouldn't have. Nothing had *changed*, not really. But I kept expecting a message from Blaine. I kept expecting some time machine to cut out the last month-plus and make things normal—comfortable—again. Kept thinking our shared experience with Nora had . . . I dunno, been a reset of some sort.

By 4:00, I finally buttoned up and opened the chat. Searched through GIFs for a solid three minutes before settling on one of a little kid peeking around a wall shyly, the word *Hi* popping up in bold white letters.

LMay: [GIF]

I waited a second for her to respond. Glanced away when Kate popped her head into the office.

"Power strips?" she asked.

"Artem stashed them under his desk while they replaced the cabinets," I answered. Our supply closet—which was more of a room than a closet—had recently gotten a makeover.

She nodded and went on her way. It wasn't until she left that I realized how clearly I'd spoken. How much I hadn't given it a second thought. Kate used to intimidate me for reasons I couldn't really name. Now she was just a colleague. Another person.

I smiled faintly to myself before turning back to the instant messenger. Not so much as a bouncing ellipsis to show Blaine was typing. She was probably working on something . . . it was normal for her to take a hot minute to reply. She couldn't possibly be so mad at me as to refuse to speak to me on messenger. Right? Right. Blaine wasn't weird like that.

I pulled up the developer salesforce page on Infrared. Glanced over it. Clicked back to the instant messenger.

If I messaged her about Infrared, she'd have to reply, yes?

Drumming my fingers on my desk, I mulled over it for a second. I hated this. Hated the feeling that this was some kind of strategy game and I didn't know all the rules. Hated that things couldn't just be easy with Blaine, like they used to be.

Maybe I should apologize. That was the right step, yes? We could just talk and work it out and it might be miserable for a minute, but the end result would be worth it.

LMay: How's Nora doing?

I was sure she'd had her baby by now, but Blaine hadn't told me anything. Seemed like she should . . . part of the reason I'd expected a message all day. But maybe she hadn't heard either. Maybe Nora was focusing on herself and her family and not on keeping her coworkers updated on every blip in her life.

I forced myself to focus on Infrared. I was successful for an entire twenty minutes before clicking back on messenger.

Nothing. I worked some magic and opened up the advanced settings. It claimed Blaine hadn't even seen my message yet.

At least she wasn't ignoring me.

I checked the clock. 4:27. She'd be down in half an hour anyway.

I pulled up my email and started filtering through the unreads.

At 4:34, I grabbed some random cables—something to do with my hands—and took the stairs up to the fourth floor.

I figured out why she wasn't responding pretty quickly upon arriving—she wasn't at her desk. The entire department was empty except for . . . Kristen. No, Kristi. I hesitated, wondering if I should go back downstairs. Kept walking—I could make a full circuit or something, or—

Blaine's laptop was gone. Was she working from home today?

I paused outside her cubicle. Didn't she usually have photos pinned on the walls? I remembered one of her and her mom at Disneyland. She had really short hair in it.

I glanced toward Kristi, catching her eye just as she looked over. "Do you know where Blaine is?"

She frowned. "She quit. Today."

A flash of cold shot through my limbs.

"HR made her leave early," she added, before leaning forward and glancing around, probably for Carol. "Honestly, good for her. I hope she finds a better job soon."

It took me a minute to work up enough spit to wet my tongue, while my stomach felt like it was drowning. "She quit?"

Kristi nodded. Glanced around again—man, she was paranoid. But I'd heard enough about her supervisor to understand why. "Carol was being ridiculous about Nora's maternity leave," she near-whispered, "and Blaine called her out on it. Then she quit." She touched a stack of papers on her desk, and the frown deepened. "Overtime for me. Sorry about your project."

"Y-Yeah." I twisted the random cables in my hands. Tried to think of something to say, but there wasn't much. I wasn't even in this department. "Thanks," I managed, and turned around, feeling awkward. Feeling like my every motion was being watched, so I hyperfocused on every movement. I glanced back when I reached the stairs. Unsurprisingly, no one noticed me. Kristi had turned back to her work.

I paused in the stairwell. Blew out hot air. *Quit.* She quit, and she didn't even tell me—

HR made her leave early. I wonder why. Then again, the culture at IO Masters was . . . something else. Maybe Carol had done something.

I mulled over this, feeling heavy, as I returned to my office. Sat down. Grabbed my mouse, but didn't do anything with it. Let go and pulled out my phone. Clicked on Blaine's contact information. Started a text—

Paused.

My mind reeled back to almost a full twenty-four hours prior, right before Blaine got the text that Nora was in trouble. To the thing she said that I hadn't gotten an opportunity to dig into, mentally or with Blaine.

The fact that you just asked me that question shows how utterly ignorant you are.

The question being why Blaine hadn't liked the old me.

Utterly ignorant. Was I ignorant? What did she mean by that?

. . . Had she?

I stared at her name on my phone. Wondered if she was okay. Erased the few letters I'd typed and started typing new ones—

Then turned the phone off and set it facedown on my desk. I pulled up the instant messenger. Went back into advanced settings and pulled up the entire history of conversations between Blaine and myself. More than two years' worth of conversations. It was a lot. I knew it'd be a lot, but I didn't think it'd be *this* a lot. It would take me forever to sift through these.

I started from the beginning, reading each message, then skimming. There was nothing notable, though I did smile— and chuckle—at a few exchanged jokes.

Five o'clock hit. Infrared time. But IO Masters had taken more than its fair share of my time lately. I wanted just a little longer to myself. To figure out how "ignorant" I apparently was.

Scroll, scroll, scroll. Pause.

> **BWickers:** It's a really great movie. I'm happy to lend it to you . . . or you could come over sometime and I'll give you the free fake director's cut.

My mouse hovered over that. First time Blaine asked me to do something outside of work. Curious, I highlighted it, along with the messages right before and after, copied, and pasted them in a document.

I kept scrolling. Passed through several complaints about Carol, more invitations to do things—a lot of them were for the café or other lunch plans. There was a conversation where I'd been feeling awkward because Aaron had made a comment about my T-shirts, and Blaine complimented my appearance. Another one where she invited me to watch *Willow* with her. Several where she asked how I was feeling, if I was okay because I seemed down. A few where I thanked her for leaving something at my desk. There were a couple where she asked if I was dating anyone . . . why would she care if I was dating anyone? Then a few where she prodded about my tabletop games and said she'd be interested in learning if I wanted to show her . . .

A sinking feeling drew down my gut as I copied and pasted, copied and pasted. Time flew by, but I remained glued to my chair, scrolling through messages.

I made it to the ones when the San Jose office was announced. *So many* messages were about me leaving for San Jose. Her saying, directly and indirectly, that she was going to miss me. Messages about how she'd asked Carol about being on the setup team, only to be turned down—which was funny, because earlier I'd passed messages about her talking about her fear of airports. There were promises of care packages. More invitations to do things . . . which I turned down. Why had I turned those down?

Had I been so insecure?

I paused scrolling again when I reached her invitation for her birthday party. Checked the date. It'd been a *month* before. Did she plan events that early, or had she wanted to ensure I could come?

Now I was getting full of myself—

Stop.

Rolling my lips together, feeling like a balloon was inflating in my chest, I copied the messages and pasted them in the document. Checked the clock—I had a meeting in twenty minutes that I couldn't miss. Kept scrolling.

> **LMay:** I'm allergic to cats.

> **BWickers:** That's okay. I don't have one.

I stared at that one for a full minute.

Wasn't that . . . flirting?

I began cranking the mouse wheel backward, rereading older messages, finding so many more like that one . . . and I copied and pasted every single one I could get to before I needed to head upstairs. Sent them to the printer.

By the time I walked to the copy machine, seventeen pages had printed, and counting.

● ○ ●

I was technically two minutes late for my meeting with Frank, Kris, and Robert Terry, the CEO of IO Masters. Frank and Robert were chatting, and Kris scrolling on his phone when I arrived. No one said anything about the time. I pulled up a seat, set up my laptop, and let its case fall to the floor, twenty-four pages of Blaine's instant messages burning a hole through it, making me antsy.

Focusing was going to be a challenge. I glanced at the clock. Nearly five—with luck, this meeting wouldn't go long.

"All right," the CEO said, calling us to order. "We have an issue with Infrared."

"Another bug?" I asked, deflating.

"With the written content we need." The VP knit his fingers together on top of the round table we'd gathered at. "We've lost *two* technical writers this week, and we already had them in short supply. We can keep working on the software, but we can't roll it out if we can't explain to sales and our customers what it does."

Frank shrugged his shoulders.

Robert pinched his nose. "All right. Is it something Eva can handle?"

Kris sighed. "No offense, but I'd want her work checked if she tried. And that requires a technical writer."

The CEO nodded. "Then we'll have to hire a contractor. I know it's a headache, but if we can get one on, this can be a done deal."

I added, softly, so as not to rile anyone, "As long as it's a contractor who's familiar with our products and systems . . ."

Frank said, "I think I could get someone caught up in a week, if they're experienced."

"Whatever you have to do." Robert glanced at Kris.

The VP leaned back in his chair and folded his arms across his chest. "First, I have to *find* a contractor. Best-case scenario, we can get documentation going in two weeks. Get him to sign an NDA and read up on what the last one—Blaine—got done. And then get more writers in-house, because this is getting ridiculous."

The CEO nodded. "I'll send down the order. Run some

numbers and see how many more we can bring on so this doesn't happen again."

My gaze shifted to my laptop bag, mentally scrolling back through all those messages. I didn't like confrontation, but I felt confident enough that I was in a position where I could be a little bolder. "I think I know what the problem is."

All three men refocused on me. "Lack of writers?"

"Yes, but," I leaned forward, propping my elbows on the desk, trying to remember Blaine's coworkers, current and past. "How many technical writer positions do we usually have?"

"Uh," the VP glanced at the CEO, who shrugged, "Four, I think?"

"Was five . . . I'm pretty sure. I'm also friends with a few of them." I did quick math in my head. "Did you know there was nearly a 100 percent turnover in that department over the last two years?"

Robert's brows drew together.

"Hiring contractors, hiring more writers, is a Band-Aid to the solution," I explained carefully. "The real problem is the supervisor."

Robert turned to Kris. "Who's the supervisor?"

"Carol," I said.

"Adams," Kris finished. "Don't know much about her."

"Blaine Wickers quit because of mistreatment via her supervisor," I stated. "Nora Patterson went into labor *in this building* because Carol pressured her to push back her maternity leave. I imagine that, if you talk to HR, you'll see her mentioned in exit interviews." I glanced at my bag, thinking back to all those messages from Blaine. "I can give you specific dates and events of harassment, if you'd like."

Robert wiped a hand down his face. "This is a mess. Hiring a new supervisor only adds to the problem."

"It's a new problem," I offered, "but stitches are better than Band-Aids."

He nodded. "I'll have someone look into it." He checked his watch. "See what you can do with Infrared in the meantime, May. We'll get you a writer as soon as we can."

* * ○

The next morning, I dropped the stack of papers on Kate's desk.

She glanced at them, then at me. "What is this?"

I felt awkward—so awkward—but I didn't know who else to ask. I didn't have any sisters, my gaming group was all guys, and I was not about to open my potential love life up to my mother. So I pushed through it and pulled over a chair. "I need a female perspective. What do you see here?"

She picked up the miniature book and glanced over the first page. I watched her face as she read. Her pale eyebrows slowly climbed higher. I expected her to complain, to spit out something like, *This isn't in my job description,* but she thumbed to the second page, eyes moving faster as she skimmed. Then the third. Skipped ahead a few and read.

"Wow," she said, but kept reading. I wondered, suddenly, if I'd broached some kind of privacy . . . but technically everything in these IMs was company-owned . . . and it was just Kate. And I needed to know just how ignorant I was. I *had* taken a Sharpie to every instance of "BWickers," though if Kate held it up to the light, she might still be able to read the screen name.

Needless to say, I didn't sleep much last night. I had those pages of messages practically memorized at that point.

Kate laughed at something, then skimmed through a couple more.

Finally, she looked up and said, "So are you going to report her to HR?"

The blood in my veins jolted at the question. I hadn't expected that. "What?"

She waved the papers like I'd forgotten their presence. "This chick is hardcore flirting with you. These obviously aren't full conversations . . . I assume you asked her to stop and she didn't."

Hardcore flirting with you. I'd thought maybe . . . I'd hoped . . . but seeing it put out there so blatantly by a third party was a weird kind of out-of-body experience. Like I'd just discovered I was on one of those hidden-camera shows. Or the lights had just been turned on at a surprise party.

Surprise! Blaine likes you.

She's always liked you.

She liked you before.

A string of half-formed curse words rolled through my mind and tempted my tongue. Blaine was right. I *was* ignorant. I *was* an ass.

I'd totally misread her in the parking lot and I'd been so tired, so mad, so *awkward*, that I hadn't heard her out.

I hadn't *heard* her for two years.

And it wasn't just that . . . it was realizing I'd put *myself* into a box of my own making. That *I'd* judged myself for how I acted, for how others perceived me, and yes, for how I looked, or at least how I *thought* I looked. Someone like Blaine had always been out of my league, but all this time, I'd been playing the wrong sport. How different would things have been right now if I hadn't been so closed off to the idea of someone like Blaine caring about me?

I'd gotten so worked up at how others treated me after my weight loss, but *I* had treated *myself* so much worse. And I needed to change that. I was changing that, so I hoped.

And Blaine. Kate was confirming what I was too scared to believe.

Blaine smiled at everyone.

But she'd smiled at me *first*. And I'd dismissed it. I'd tucked it away and schooled myself into "reason" and *ignored her* for two years . . .

"Lysander?" Kate snapped her fingers in front of my face, bringing me back to the present.

One of those curse words snuck past my lips.

Kate blinked. "Are you okay? Do you want *me* to report her?"

"Wh-What?" I shook myself. Gathered the papers. "No. No. This is . . . this is a good thing."

She cocked an eyebrow. "This isn't the writer gal, is it? The brunette?"

Blood drained from my face. How did she guess?

I wasn't *that* oblivious, was I?

Oh God help me. I was, wasn't I?

"I need to go," I mumbled, and pushed the extra chair back into its cubicle. I checked my watch. I'd been at work a whole fifteen minutes.

"Go where?" Kate asked.

"I'm taking a day," I said, oddly shaky. "Um. You guys have enough to do, right?"

She looked at me like I'd grown a second head. "Do we ever *not* have enough to do?"

"Right. Okay." I gave her an awkward thumbs-up, but my mind was too caught up in the glaring evidence in my hands that my anxiety didn't troll me with the awkward gesture. I marched back to my office and grabbed my computer bag. Barely remembered to shove my laptop in it before leaving.

She must be so pissed at me, I thought as I booked it for the stairs, walking as quickly as I could without jogging. *I have to make it up to her.*

But how?

Well, I'd just given myself a full eight-hour shift to figure it out.

Chapter 14

BLAINE

I SAT AT my kitchen counter, booty in barstool, hunched over my computer. Looking for a full-time job was a full-time job. My forearms were cold from the granite, but I was too lazy to go into my room for a sweater. I'd slept in this morning and taken my sweet time checking social media and my news feeds, then I made myself an enormous breakfast and updated my résumé with an end date for IO Masters.

It was a little frightening, to type those numbers in there, yet incredibly satisfying. Kind of like trying boba tea for the first time.

I searched Utah jobs for a couple hours, then spent another writing personalized cover letters for each, which thoroughly burned out my brain cells. Fortunately, my Netflix subscription and DoorDash had just the remedy I needed. Then I called my mom for an hour and got back on the computer, this time searching for jobs in Eastern Washington.

There weren't as many, but I wasn't a quitter.

I was on my eighth cover letter when the side door opened and shut—that was the door over the stairs that led to Rue's chunk of the house. However, Rue came strolling into the kitchen, her wrists laden with grocery bags and a Tootsie Pop in her mouth. "I found out the most amazing thing today."

I finished my sentence before glancing up. "Oh?"

"You can order crickets. *In the mail.*"

I waited for the punch line. She dropped her groceries on the counter and pushed now-red hair out of her face. Took a long suck on the lollipop and plucked it from her mouth. "Live crickets, Blaine. Like for iguanas and stuff. And you can *mail them to people.*"

A chuckle stairwayed up my throat. "Oh dear."

She pulled up a stool. "I have so many people I could mail crickets to." Whipping out her phone, she pulled up her contacts. "I just don't have addresses for all of them. But that's what the internet is for." She glanced at me. "What's Carol's last name?"

I snorted. "We are not mailing Carol crickets."

"*We* don't have to. *I* can." She waggled her eyebrows.

I laughed. "I'd rather send them to Chad anyway."

"Which Chad?" she asked. I'd of course told her about my escort out of IO Masters.

I considered for a moment. "Both."

"Both it is." She opened up a list app on her phone and wrote the name "Chad" twice, plus a few others—I recognized Lindsay, her old roommate, and Landry, a guy who'd ghosted her a few years back. Maybe she just butted heads with *L*-names.

Next on the list was Lysander.

"Don't mail Lysander crickets," I said, the mirth trickling out of my voice. I could feel a headache blooming between my eyes, so I shut my laptop. "Lysander is fine. Lysander saved Nora."

"Questionable," she countered.

I shrugged. "It's better that I moved on anyway." I ran my hand over my computer. "Maybe literally."

Rue deflated. "I really hope you find somewhere nearby. I don't want you to move out of state."

I smiled at her. Rue had always been so supportive, without being overbearing. "I probably won't. Utah just has more jobs, unless I move to Seattle." But Seattle was on the other side of the state from Mom, so what was the point? "I don't know." I pulled off my computer glasses. "Maybe Utah isn't for me."

I wondered what would happen on Hooked if I changed my location to the Palouse. If it would even matter, because I hadn't even opened the app in . . . I couldn't remember. A while.

A quick knock sounded at the door. "Probably the Tupperware I ordered." I lived for Amazon Prime.

Rue chucked her lollipop over the counter into the trash can. Girl always did have good coordination—that was what made her such a good jammer. "I'll grab it and then take this stuff downstairs." She gestured to the grocery bags. "Movie night?"

"In or out?"

She shrugged and ventured to the door.

I drummed my fingers on my laptop. Out might be good for me. I had a feeling I was going to be indoors hunching over job applications for a while. I still hadn't heard back from the ones I'd interviewed for.

What was playing? I pulled out my phone and went to my movie app to check.

"I'm going downstairs!" Rue shouted. Thumping footsteps announced her departure.

I glanced up. "Okay . . . ?" She'd left her groceries here, and I'd guess the package inside the door. Maybe she needed to take a call—

And suddenly flowers entered my kitchen. A giant bouquet of summer flowers, and a second bouquet of red roses, with legs. I froze, hand hovering over the latest M. Night Shyamalan film, as a face popped up above the blooms.

Lysander.

My heart stopped. Literally stopped. For half a second, I saw the tunnel and the light. Then I blinked, and it was gone, and my lungs strained for air as they coerced my most important organ back to work.

"Wh-Wh-What are you doing here?" I asked, standing, then unsure, sitting again. Lysander moved forward and dumped the flowers—and several other things—on the counter.

"I . . . sorry, I didn't know what to get at the store." He fumbled with the unexpected treasures, not meeting my eyes. "Flowers are obvious." He grabbed the rose bouquet and handed it to me; I took it tentatively as my skin buzzed and brain rang through a variety of silent alarms with no meaning or purpose. "I wasn't sure what you'd want." He spoke quickly, obviously nervous, though he didn't stutter. "Candy." He thrust a bag of assorted chocolates my direction.

"A card . . . but I haven't written in it yet." He set a teal card with a silver embossed dove and the words *I'm sorry* aside. "And, uh, eggs." He pulled up a carton of them. "I don't know why I got eggs. Do you need eggs?"

I only realized my mouth was hanging open when my tongue started to dry out, but even then, it took an effort to close it.

My silence made him squirm for a few seconds, but then he lit up. "Also, I might be getting Carol fired."

"Wh-What?" I sat up straight. "How . . . Why?" I gestured to the offerings. "Why all of this?"

A thriving bead of hope pulsed in the back of my rib cage.

Lysander gripped the counter. "Because of how I acted." He finally met my eyes, and the depth of his sent an electric shock straight through my face and into my navel. "I read through all our messages. Very thoroughly. And you're right—I was really ignorant. And bad at communicating. And I'm really sorry." He picked up the other bouquet. Paused. Set it down. "I really hope I wasn't one of the reasons you quit."

A . . . sound . . . emitted from me. I supposed I could liken it to a giggle. A sort of childish, manic giggle that scratched my windpipe all the way up. "I, uh . . . you're forgiven." *Is this really happening?* Stuff like this only happened in romance novels. "And no, I quit because Carol is Satan incarnate. And if you get her fired, you are my savior."

A small smile perked up his lip, and it was literally the most handsome I'd ever seen him. That shock swirled around my navel and threatened to cut me in half. Another giggle was building in my chest, and I knew it'd be loud and weird if I let it out.

"Good," he managed. Backed away from the counter.

Wrung his hands, then stuck them in his pockets, then wrung them again.

"So we're good?" I asked, at the same time he said, "I like you too."

The tail end of my question dribbled down my lips. "Wh-What?"

He took a deep breath. "I like you too." His eyes dropped to the chocolates. "I never asked you out because I wrote you off as impossible really early in our friendship and I never really got over that. I mean, the writing-off. Of you. Not like I'm over *you*." He wiped a hand across his forehead and cursed under his breath. "I practiced this in the car. This sounded a lot better in the car."

New alarms sang between my ears. I clutched the bouquet, slowly strangling the roses within their cellophane wrapping. Helium slowly replaced my blood and my cheeks were already starting to hurt from a grin he didn't even see, because he wasn't looking at me. Because it was easier not to look, for stuff like this. Even for an extrovert.

"I look different now," he continued, motioning nonsense with his hands, "and I thought that was what you liked, and it's not and . . . I'm still a little insecure. I'm working on it." He met my eyes, looking startled for an instant. Probably at my Joker-esque grin. But his face was all seriousness, so my expression sobered.

Looking me dead in the eyes, he added, "I might not always look like this. Sometimes I'm too tired to go to the gym, especially with projects like Infrared. I haven't been in two weeks." He ran a hand back through his hair. "Sometimes I'll eat a whole pizza in one sitting—"

"Lysander," I said, and he paused. "I literally do not care

how many pizzas you eat, period. Or how many muscle-monkey friends you make at the gym."

That little smile twitched his lips. I wanted to kiss it. Know what it tasted like. But I was about to float right off this chair. My fingers and feet were buzzing with this strange sort of elation . . . not like anything I'd ever felt before.

And we just stared at each other for several seconds, me buzzing, him . . . I don't know, but it seemed like something good.

Finally, I cleared my throat. "So are you going to ask me out or not?"

His shoulders slackened with what looked like relief. And I was floating, right off that stool. Bouncing around the ceiling like a forgotten party balloon—

"Yes. Yes, I am asking you out."

I liked being a balloon. "For right now?"

"Um." He checked his watch. "Yes? Yes. Are you free right now . . . ?"

I was pretty sure Rue would forgive me missing our half-formed movie date. I set the roses down on the counter. "I am very ready now." I glanced down at my sweats. "Uh . . . give me ten? I'd like to dress to impress."

He was smiling now, full-on smile, and my balloon-self threatened to burst. "You don't need to . . . but yeah. Yeah, go ahead. Whatever you want."

I almost said, *I want you,* but I didn't want to push my luck.

Because at that moment, I was the luckiest woman in all of Happy Valley.

○ ● ●

It was surreal, walking out of my house with Lysander. The October sun had set, but it wasn't too cold. He opened my door for me with a shy smile, and that shyness reverberated in my chest, making me feel like I was fourteen again and going to my first dance. I slid into the Camry, he sat next to me, and we were off.

And it was like none of it ever happened.

"I watched *Willow*," he said as he turned onto the main road.

I perked up. "You did? Did you like it?"

He chuckled. "It was pure trunky fantasy. Of course I liked it. But I will definitely watch it again with fake director's commentary."

That comment spurred an old memory, and it took me a second to place it. "Did I say that, once? Fake director's commentary?"

He nodded.

I stared at him for a second. "You really read through all our instant messages? How are you not ninety years old right now?"

He smiled, and that smile was all for me, and it raised goose bumps up my legs and arms, prickling around fading derby bruises. "Plastic surgery."

I pushed his shoulder as we pulled up to a light. "Your doctor is incredible."

There's this thing in Happy Valley, right at the north end of it, called Thanksgiving Point. Old farmland, I think, that was converted into showrooms and shops and pretty landscaping. In April they have a tulip festival; in December, a Christmas-light extravaganza. In between, just pretty stuff to see. Lysander pulled in there, not knowing I could use some outdoors, as well as a walk to release this shy, nervous energy building in me. But maybe he needed that too.

Because he'd brought me flowers. And chocolates. And . . . eggs. And said he liked me too, and I was *on a date with Lysander May* and what even was the universe?

He bought us some fancy-pants paper wrist-straps, and we walked into the gardens, which were still bright with fall colors, illuminated by well-placed lamps along a paver path. Something smelled good, like final blooms and petrichor. Taking a deep breath, I caught Lysander's L'Homme cologne and wondered if he'd sprayed on extra for me.

And then Lysander did something I would never have guessed he'd do. At least, not that he'd initiate.

He held my hand.

I grinned like a hound driving down the freeway with its face hanging out the window. Full jowls.

He noticed and laughed. "What?"

"You."

"You what?"

That insane giggle was forming in my throat again. Turning into a ten-year-old, I sang, "You *liiiike* me."

He laughed and rolled his eyes. "We've established this."

I squeezed his hand. It was the perfect kind of hand-holding hand—warm and dry and sized just right. "You know what they say about big hands?"

The slightest sobering overtook his expression. "What?"

"Big gloves."

He shoved me gently, like he had after showing me his amazing butt tattoo, but since our fingers were securely tethered together, I came bouncing right back. Right against his side, and I didn't have to apologize or step back, and it was *wonderful* and I was ballooning all over again.

"What happened with Carol?" he asked, and I dramatically told him about the morning meeting—tangenting to include what I knew about Nora and her new baby boy—and the awkward HR escort. And how I had to send Kristi back up for his pen.

"I'm glad you didn't burn it," he said.

"Does resin burn?"

"I'm glad you didn't . . . melt it," he amended.

I leaned my head on his shoulder—I'd been wanting to for *so freaking long*—for a minute, until the path turned and I had to straighten out. "Sorry about Infrared."

"No more work talk." He thought for a moment. "Favorite supervillain."

"Have we had this conversation before?"

He shrugged.

I thought for a moment. "Carol Adams."

He laughed. "*No work talk!*"

I thought again. "Maybe Galaxia from *Sailor Moon*. She was pretty bad-A."

"*Sailor Moon?* The anime?"

I shrugged. "Teenaged me was very into *Sailor Moon*."

So we talked about villains, and comics, and *Willow*, and *Lord of the Rings* and what ice cream flavors Middle Earth might possibly have, and of course the whole eagles-and-the-Ring theory that's been discussed to death but still bears pertinence. And we planned a *Lord of the Rings* director's cut marathon for Saturday, and I was elated because my chaste fantasy of cuddling Lysander on a couch was less than twenty-four hours away from becoming reality.

I was hound-smiling again, and the temperature had dropped enough to make my teeth hurt when I did it.

We reached a koi pond and stopped on a bridge to peer into the water. "Are they still in there?" I asked.

"Must be. I doubt they scoop them all out for winter storage. Maybe just down deeper." He checked his pockets. Pulled out a stick of gum. "Think they like gum?"

"I think we'll get kicked out if we feed the fish gum." But a jittery idea sprung to mind, and I plucked the stick out of his hand, unwrapped it, and popped it in my mouth. Raised an eyebrow. "Spearmint?"

He leaned his elbow on the bridge railing. "What's wrong with spearmint?"

Shaking my head, I said, "Wintergreen, Ly. *Wintergreen* is the king of gums."

"Not tutti-frutti?"

"Ew." I chewed quickly, wanting to freshen up. I could feel my pulse in my fingertips, and not from the cold. I tried to give him "the look"—you know, that under-the-eyelashes things girls do in movies. Face flirting, essentially. "Have you ever noticed, in fantasy movies, all the romantic stuff happens on a bridge?"

That sobering happened again. He totally looked at my lips. *Yes. Lips. And gum. Hopefully, we have mastered the art of taking a hint.*

"Oh?" He sounded, somehow, confident and nervous at the same time.

I nodded. "Aragorn and Arwen, for example."

He thought for a moment. "They kissed on a bridge?"

"The necklace thing."

He thought. "Wasn't that on, like . . . a giant tree branch? Or a deck?"

I laughed. "Do elves have decks?"

"I believe decks are signs of ecological advancement, so they must."

I stomped my foot. "Oh my gosh, will you just kiss me, please?"

He leaned back and laughed nervously. "Thus the gum."

"We must put the gum to good use."

He had a moment—just a sliver of time—to start leaning forward before a shrill voice said, "Mommy! Fish!" Followed by pattering on the bridge as a kid, maybe seven years old, ran past us, grabbing the railing right behind Lysander. A mom pushing a stroller was coming up the path.

Lysander ran a hand down his face. "I'm going to push that kid into the water."

I laughed and took his hand in both of mine, pulling him away from the railing. We crossed the rest of the bridge, then stepped off the path onto the grass where a couple pine trees stood. I readied my next witty remark, but as I turned toward Lysander, his hand came up to cup my jaw and his lips pressed into mine.

Pop. Pop-pop-pop. A million internal balloons exploded all at once. Every brain alarm sang and shrilled. Every bump that could possibly goose on my skin goosed *hard*, and chills swept up my spine and danced in my hair while heat pulsed in my lips.

This. This moment was literally what I'd been created for. Maybe it was all the waiting, maybe it was the connection we had, but something about kissing Lysander awoke every inch of my body and sealed every crack in my heart. High school dances, bars, and YouTube ceased to exist. It was just Lysander, like it had always been Lysander. Like I hadn't been waiting two years for him, but all thirty, and this was the brilliant climax in a movie all our own.

I wrapped my arms around his neck and kissed him, tasting him, savoring the feel of his short beard against my skin and his other hand finding my waist. I *fit* here. I *belonged* here. Tangled there with Lysander May was . . . home.

We pulled apart, barely able to see each other between the night sky and the looming pine trees. I stared up into the majestic near-black eyes. *How is this real?*

"You have really nice hamstrings," he murmured.

I blinked. Laughed. "Wait, what?"

And then I got to hear the story of the retrieved thumb drive and my magical sequin shorts as we continued winding through the gardens. And the story of the awkward neighbor setup. I reciprocated with Operation Blaine's Thirtieth Birthday. All the while we walked hand in hand, and every time we crossed a bridge, we pulled close and exchanged a kiss, each one just as explosive as the first.

And everything in the world was right and perfect.

Chapter 15

LYSANDER

AND JUST LIKE that, everything changed.

I spent all weekend with Blaine. We stayed out until the gardens closed, then got frozen yogurt and chatted in neon chairs around a small table until that place closed too. I drove her home, and we talked in the driveway until three in the morning.

I am not a night owl. But I had a feeling that was quickly going to change.

Saturday, I showed up at 10:00 a.m. Blaine made me breakfast. *Healthy* breakfast. After some sleuthing, I figured out she'd gone to the grocery store that morning, despite staying up so late, to make sure she had things I'd feel comfortable eating. I'd meant what I said—sometimes I just wanted a piece of pizza. Sometimes I worried I'd lose my reins on my health, though I was working hard to prevent that. But the subtle show of support meant a lot to me.

Normally, I would consider it sacrilege to make out through half of *The Two Towers*, but in all honesty, it was the best viewing of *The Lord of the Rings* I'd ever had.

During a bathroom break, I deleted Hooked from my phone.

We had another late night, then a hike up American Fork Canyon and a picnic lunch on Sunday. We talked about new tattoos we could get. We talked about our families. We talked about Vision from the Marvel movies versus the comics. And in truth, it felt like it had always been Blaine. It was so *easy* with Blaine.

Best weekend of my life.

It sucked not having Blaine at IO Masters, but I guess the spat we'd had got me accustomed to not having her username pop up on my screen all the time. I just texted her instead, and I had an app on my phone that gave me way more GIF options than the instant messaging service did.

> **Me:** VP's pretty frantic. Already have interviews tomorrow for tech writers.

> **Blaine:** Already? Wow.
> How do you know?

> **Me:** They want me in on them. Want to hire someone who can get started on Infrared immediately.
> [GIF of a fist slamming a red button]
> How's the job hunt?

> **Blaine:** Same as usual. I actually did get an offer today . . . in Moscow. Idaho, not Russia.

But, uh . . . I will be turning it down.
For reasons.

Me: Hopefully good reasons.

Blaine: You are a good kisser, so.
;)

I chuckled and found a GIF of a monkey blushing. Sent it.

Me: I can ask around.

Blaine: Thanks! I don't want to drive farther than
SLC, but I might have to look at, barf, Ogden.

Me: Listen. I'll hire you to clean my house.
Ten-minute commute. Easy.

Blaine: You punk.
There are easier ways to get me into your bedroom,
you know.

I laughed as my face heated, glad no one was witnessing it.
A soft knock on the office door had me jumping in my
chair and dropping my phone. It was Frank.

"Hey." He rubbed his eyes—it wasn't even lunchtime and
the guy looked exhausted. "We have a bug with one of the
portals. I've got a guy on it, but it might set us back."

Letting out a sigh, I pushed my chair back from the desk.
"Okay, thanks." I eyed him. "Do you want me to talk to Kris
about getting another developer?"

Frank dropped his hand and chuckled. "You think I *haven't* talked to Kris about getting more guys on my team?"

I considered this a moment. "He might be more amenable, with the tech writer crisis. He might be willing to take on a contractor."

Frank nodded slowly. "All right, yeah. See what he says. Thanks." He turned to leave, but paused. "You seem awfully chipper, all things considering."

"Do I?" I picked up my phone and set it behind my computer tower.

"Yeah." He eyed me. "Whatever you're doing, keep doing it. It's nice to have some cheer when crap's hitting the fan."

He gave me a thumbs-up and walked away.

Scooping up my phone, I texted Blaine back.

Me: [GIF of cartoon waggling eyebrows]

Blaine: You need better game. Totally used that one before.

Me: Have I?

Blaine: [Same GIF of cartoon waggling eyebrows]

I laughed.

Blaine: Dinner tonight?

I sighed.

Me: Unfortunately, overtime is starting to look like

my new normal. Hoping to get some more developers too. Gotta talk to VP. And by talk, I mean beg.
[GIF of peasant man begging]

Blaine: Bleh. Sorry. That sucks.

Me: [GIF of man shrugging]
It is what it is. But they'll never take my weekends
from me.
[GIF of medieval general leading a charge]

Setting down my phone, I got back to work. Maybe if
I could focus and really put my head down, I could get out
early enough to see Blaine for a couple hours before I had to
turn in. Staying up late on the weekends was one thing, but I
couldn't pull it off on weekdays. Not if I wanted to function.

I sent an email to Kris Kenger's assistant, asking for a
meeting time, preferably that afternoon.

● ○ ●

I wasn't sure what it was. A case of the Mondays, too much
overtime getting to my head, or all the problems with Infrared
piling one after another after another, but by the time five
o'clock dragged itself onto my watch, I was beat. My brain
felt like it was full of cotton candy, my eyelids were heavy
as train cars, and my butt was numb from sitting. And I had
another three, maybe four hours of this.

Sighing, I closed my files and unplugged my laptop from
its monitors. Until we had a technical writer, I could just do
my work from my office. Frank didn't need me too often, so

it wasn't a big deal. But a change of scenery might help jog my brain cells, as would a walk to the café. They closed at six, so best if I didn't dawdle.

Laptop under my arm, I trekked to the Infrared cubicles, passing Frank as I went down the aisle. He had a plastic bowl of what looked like chow mein in his hands and a smile on his face.

"Smells good!" he said, and I didn't entirely grasp what he meant.

Until I reached the last cubicle on the right, the one Blaine and I had shared. I blinked, making sure I was seeing straight and not just imagining that she was standing there.

She stood out, because she wasn't in dress code—she had a Pokémon T-shirt on and ripped jeans, and her hair was curled so electric blue tangled through the brown. And there was an array of Tupperware set out on the desk, along with more plastic bowls like the one Frank had been carrying.

"Ta-da," she offered with a shy smile, which was so rare for her, yet so captivating. "I'll just stay long enough to eat, but legally you get a break right now, so . . . Chinese is happening."

I laughed, incredulous, eyes going from her to the food. "This is . . . amazing." I paused. "How did you get in?"

She shrugged. "The receptionist likes me. And it's after hours, so."

Crossing the cramped cubicle space, I put my arms around her shoulders and squeezed her tight. Her hair smelled like something floral. My thumb traced the hidden raven tattoo.

"Thank you," I said into her curls. "This is really nice. Thank you."

She squeezed me, then pulled back and looked at me. "I also brought cake. It's in that bag." She tilted her head, and I noticed a white paper bag under the desk. "You can choose whether or not you want it. I don't want to mess with your thing. But also, I brought cake."

I laughed, and I knew I was still at work, but I hugged her again, not really caring if anyone spied us over the short cubicle walls. And not just because she also brought me dessert. But because that cake meant something. It meant she really did like *me*. She liked me if I ate cake, and she liked me if I didn't. And that simple act of love made me feel like all of it was worth it.

I really felt like I could have my cake and eat it too.

● ● ○

BLAINE

I jammed my brake into the floor and pinned my knee against Emily's, keeping the American Pitch Forks' jammer from slipping by us on the inside edge of the track. She pushed, keeping her hands by her collarbone so she wouldn't foul, but it wasn't enough. Shifting my weight, I bumped her hip with mine, which was just enough force to skate her over the line. The referee blew his whistle, and the jammer, with a dramatic eyeroll, skated back down the track to try again.

Emily whooped and high-fived me as we readied ourselves for another go. The game was tight—if we won this, we'd go to the midwestern finals. The Salt Lake Sinners were two points ahead.

I glanced up in the stands before the whistle blew again, to where Lysander sat near the center aisle. He definitely wasn't at the point where he felt comfortable screaming or waving a sign around a bunch of strangers, but he was there, clapping as the jammer started for us again. I grinned. How long had I daydreamed of him being there? Was this even real?

The other blockers shifted, calling my attention back to the game. The jammer came at us with renewed vigor, this time trying to drill right down the center. Emily shifted toward Yolanda to cut her off; I supported Emily, who was our smallest blocker, so the jammer couldn't nudge her aside.

Yolanda twisted, and the jammer fell on the waxed floor. I thought that was that, but the jammer started hand-signaling a time-out with a grimace on her face, and I realized she'd hurt herself. How, I wasn't sure. I skated over to grab her under her shoulder while Emily got her other. She favored her right leg. Damn. Injuries could knock a person off the team for good, if they were bad enough. Otherwise, this gal might be out for the rest of the season . . . or her team might forfeit, since it was so small it didn't have any extra people. I hated winning by forfeit.

We helped the jammer back to her bench, where her teammates and the volunteer EMT took over. I skated back to my team's bench, waiting for a call.

Rue, who'd pulled off her skates, said, "Your phone has been buzzing like crazy." She snatched it from the bench and handed it to me. "Who's Paul?"

I froze. Even the wheels on my skates didn't budge.

Paul was my dad. He and my mom had split when I was a teenager—he'd remarried quickly after and moved to South Dakota. I didn't see him much—he called on Christmas, and we called him on Father's Day, more out of routine than anything else.

He never called me out of the blue. Never.

Hands sweaty, I unlocked my phone and saw *thirteen* missed calls. Eight from my dad, five from Tess—my younger sister who lived in Virginia with her husband.

My stomach dropped. I skated away from the bench, across the track, and past the bleachers. Lysander was standing and caught my eye—I held up a "one minute" finger and sailed past the two vendors we had today, down the hallway, and into the bathroom.

I called Tess.

"Blaine!" she shouted as she answered on the second ring. "Blaine, where the hell are you?"

I held on to one of the sinks. "I'm at derby. What's wrong?"

"Derby, right." She took a shuddering breath. "Mom's in the hospital."

My right skate gave out from under me. Back hitting the cold tile wall, I gripped the sink and slid down ungracefully to my butt, chills devouring me like hungry spiders. "What do you mean?"

Tess's voice choked as she spoke. "She's had an aneurysm."

I gasped, hand flying to my mouth. "A stroke?"

"I don't know. I don't think so. He said"—I heard the sound of flipping paper— "A thoracic aortic aneurysm. She's in surgery right now."

"Oh no." Tears welled in my eyes, and my throat grew thick. "Is she okay?"

"She's in surgery, Blaine."

"How'd she get there?"

"I don't know. *I don't know.*" She sniffed, and we both paused, trying to control ourselves. "I guess Dad was still listed as her emergency contact. He's on a work trip in Florida." Another pause. I bit the meat of my palm and blinked rapidly. The referee's whistle echoed down the hallway, probably calling a forfeit game. "I can try to come out, but I have the kids—"

"No, no, I don't have kids or a job. I'll go." I put her on speaker and, after wiping tears from my eyes, pulled up plane tickets on my phone. Planes to Palouse had to route through Spokane since its airport was so tiny. Even *Spokane's* airport was tiny.

"You don't have a job?"

"No, I quit." It came out as a whisper as a hedgehog-size lump settled itself midthroat. I booked a red-eye for tonight. "It's okay. It's meant to be. I'll call you back, okay? If you hear anything else—"

"I'll call Dad and tell him you're going."

I pulled myself onto my skates. "Have him call the hospital and change the emergency contact to me, okay?" My voice was croaking by now. How Tess understood me, I wasn't sure.

"Okay. Okay." Breath. "Love you. Bye."

"Bye." I didn't have pockets, so I shoved my phone between my sweaty boobs and skated back to the door.

When I wrenched it open, Lysander was on the other side, phone to his ear. Mine started buzzing, then stopped when he hung up. He straightened and stiffened when he saw my face.

"What's wrong?" He grabbed my elbow to support me. My balance on eight wheels was pretty spectacular, but I was definitely shaky right then. "Blaine, what happened?"

I swallowed. "I need to go to Palouse." Half whisper, half croak. "My mom had an aneurysm. No one else is up there with her."

He stared, dumbfounded, for about half a second before nodding. "Okay, okay. When?"

"Red-eye. Tonight." I swallowed. "I need to take off these skates."

He stepped back, and I lowered myself to the floor, ignoring a few stairs as our audience started filtering toward the front doors. As I unlaced my right skate, Lysander unlaced my left. Then jumped to his feet and ran back into the gymnasium. But the time I pulled my skates and helmet off, he'd returned with my shoes and duffel bag.

"I'll drive you," he said. "Help you pack."

"It's okay." I wiped my eyes again.

"I'll drive you." He helped me to my feet. Escorted me the rest of the way to the doors. By the time we reached the parking lot, urgency replaced my shock. I had four hours until my plane left. The airport was a forty-five-minute drive. I'd want to get there at least an hour early—

"But my car," I said as we reached his.

"We'll take care of it."

I got inside. Spied through the back windshield Rue running out; Lysander must have explained things very quickly, because they only spoke for about twenty seconds before Rue ran back inside. Then Lysander got behind the wheel and drove me home. Had a cop been watching, he would have earned himself at least three various traffic violations.

Everything kind of blurred together after that. Lysander pulled into my driveway and hadn't quite stopped when

I bolted out of the car and into the house, unlocking the door with a keycode. In my bedroom, I searched my closet, then under my bed, for my suitcase. Threw it on my bed and started packing, trying to think of how many pairs of underwear I might need and *Why is Mom in the hospital what kind of surgery is she going to survive what will I do if I get "the call"?*

Shirts. Pants. Underwear. I ran to the bathroom. Deodorant. Hair stuff? Maybe just the straightener. I could buy anything I needed. Ponytails were an option. Toothbrush—toothpaste. Did I need shampoo? Probably not.

Back in my room, I circled the space a few times, trying to think of what I might need. Oh! Phone charger. Laptop and charger. A pen? Did I need a pen? I threw it in my suitcase anyway.

"What flight are you on?"

"Huh?" I spun around, but Lysander had called from the kitchen. I chucked a hastily thrown together makeup bag into my suitcase and zipped it before pulling out my phone. "383 to Palouse," I said, and shoved it in my pocket. Paused, remembering shoes. I should have another pair of shoes. I grabbed some boots from my closet and rolled my suitcase into the hallway.

Lysander met me with a Saran-Wrapped sandwich. "Here."

I took the sandwich, stared at it, and started bawling.

"Hey. Hey." Lysander's warm arms came around my shoulders, and I cried into his collar. "It's okay. You're going to make it. She's going to be okay."

I shook my head. "You don't know that."

"If she's half as stubborn as you are, she'll pull through."

I laugh-cried against his neck. Pulled back and wiped various liquids from my face. Lysander kissed my forehead.

"Let's go." He took my suitcase and pulled me toward the door. Saw me inside the Camry before running back inside and returning with a roll of toilet paper, since I was too cheap for Kleenex.

And I cried all over again.

Chapter 16

LYSANDER PULLED IN to covered parking and pulled my suitcase out of the trunk for me. I insisted I could take it—which might have come out as half-audible mumbles—but he held on to its handle with one hand and my hand with the other, and I was so, *so* grateful he was there when I got the call. That he was there to help me. That he was there to keep me in one piece, at least until I got on the plane.

I hated airports.

We took a crosswalk into the terminal, me staring at the ceiling and blinking rapidly so as not to draw attention to my undoubtedly red face and puffy eyes. I checked my phone for what had to be the thirtieth time, but there were no new calls or texts. No new information. Mom was in surgery—however long that might take. I imagined a long time, for a ruptured artery. We wouldn't know anything until it was over.

We'd nearly reached security when Lysander's phone rang. He paused, released the suitcase, and answered it. "You here?"

I paused, wondering what he meant.

Lysander turned around, then waved at a guy running from the other direction. He had a black duffel bag slung over his shoulder with a Captain America shield embroidered on it. Lysander hung up, and the guy ran up to us, breathing hard.

"Here." He handed the bag over. "You owe me."

My gaze darted between the two. "What's going on?"

"This is Jose, one of my gaming buddies," Lysander said as he scrolled through his phone.

I waved weakly. "Hi."

Bent over, panting, with his hands on his knees, Jose nodded. "Hey."

Lysander then turned his phone screen to me, a white plane ticket appearing there. "Flight 383 to Palouse."

It took a solid three seconds for me to process. "Wait, what? You bought a ticket?" All the butterflies swirled in my stomach, pressing through its walls to flutter around my ribs and intestine too.

He nodded. "If that's okay."

I pinched my lips together, trying not to cry again. Blinked. "But Infrared—"

"Is stalled anyway, and I have a lot of PTO saved up. It can wait."

New tears leaked from my eyes. I hugged him, despite the late-night airport crowd and Jose watching. He embraced me back, not trying to rush me, just holding me until I was ready.

I loved this man.

"Okay, well," Jose chimed in after a moment, "I'm heading back. You owe me."

"The bag of holding is yours," Lysander said over my shoulder.

I heard a rustle of clothing as Jose did what I assumed to be a motion of victory. By the time I pulled back, he was gone.

"He's a nice friend." I wiped my eyes with my knuckle.

Lysander smiled at me. "He is."

I swallowed, but that lump in my throat was growing roots. "I really hate airports," I whispered.

"I know." He took my hand, and my suitcase, and we passed through security together.

○ ● ●

Mom was okay.

Not pristine—but okay. The surgery was successful, so I was told at six in the morning Pacific time in the hospital waiting room, half asleep on Lysander's shoulder while *Willow* played on his phone. The doctor told me to expect a new normal: Mom would need four to six weeks to recover from the surgery, and her chance for a heart attack and stroke had significantly increased. She was to have several follow-up appointments to ensure her kidneys were okay, because the doctor was worried there might be damage to them as well.

No warning signs. Not that I knew of. And now my mom was in a hospital bed.

I didn't want to leave before she woke, so Lysander and I had breakfast in the hospital cafeteria, then tried to get comfortable on the waiting room couch and catch a few Zs. Around eleven, a nurse came to fetch me. Mom was awake, but hooked up on oxygen and all kinds of other tubes and machines. Somehow, I had not run out of eye water yet, so I sat by her, smoothed back her half-gray hair, and talked at her, since she couldn't really talk back. I told her what had happened and how I got there. In return, I gleaned that she was surprised to see me and she felt like a pile of horse crap.

She fell back asleep. Only then did Lysander and I, in a rented car, drive to her house in the Palouse, where we crashed for a couple hours before packing her a bag and driving back to the hospital. Lysander never complained, even once. He took a couple calls for work. Otherwise, he was my pillar, and I was glad I didn't have to weed through the emotions of this alone.

Mom met Lysander on day three of seven in the hospital. She was off oxygen, and though she was weak, she looked more herself. When Lysander walked in, she said, "Well, it's about damn time."

I smiled, Lysander pulled up a seat, and they talked for about an hour while a documentary on tiny houses played on the overhead TV.

After a week, Mom was released from the hospital, and two days later, on Halloween, Lysander had to get back to Utah. I couldn't drive him to the airport—I was too afraid to leave my mom—so we said a long farewell on my mom's doorstep, and he took the rental car back to the airport.

And I cried some more.

● ○ ●

LYSANDER

At least at IO Masters, things were starting to run smoothly again.

They hired a technical writer while I was away and were

in the final interview process for another. I'd approved a contractor that morning to help Frank. Overtime would resume this evening, and we had a lot of catching up to do. I wasn't looking forward to it.

The normal workday was nearly over when I checked my phone yet again. Blaine hadn't texted me since early this morning. Ever since our reconciliation, she kept up with me just as often, if not more often, than she had on the company's instant messenger. I'd nearly chewed a hole through my lip worrying.

> **Me:** Everything OK?
> [GIF of child looking through keyhole]
> Hey, do you need anything?

I'd just finished saving new files to my thumb drive when my phone buzzed in my pocket. The second I saw Blaine's name on the screen, I left my office and strode toward the stairwell for some privacy.

"Hey," I answered as the door shut behind me. "You okay? How's your mom?"

She didn't answer at first—I checked to make sure I hadn't dropped the call. But I heard a sniff.

"Blaine?"

"Sh-She needs dialysis," she said, voice raw and quiet. "Three times a week until she's ready for another procedure."

I let out a long breath and leaned against the wall. "Oh man, that sucks. That . . . really sucks."

Another long pause. "She doesn't have anyone to take her to dialysis."

I think my body knew where the conversation was going

before my brain did. Everything inside me grew heavy and began tugging toward the floor.

"I don't know how long"—she paused—"she'll need the help. But my sister can't move her family to Washington. And"—another pause, punctuated by a shuddering breath—"and I got a job offer at the University of Idaho. Marketing. Pays pretty good. Thirty-minute drive . . ."

I ran a hand down my face. Replanted my feet to keep myself upright.

Blaine wasn't coming back.

"You have to do what's right for her," I said quietly. Footsteps echoed in the stairwell above me but disappeared onto another floor.

"Yeah." She sniffed. Hesitated. "This sucks."

"Yeah, it sucks."

"I just . . ." She took nearly a full minute to compose herself. I could see her in my mind's eye, sitting at the farm-style kitchen table at her mom's house, bent over in a chair with her brown-and-blue hair falling to either side of her, bare feet pushing into the hardwood floor. "I just finally got you, you know?"

The walls of my throat thickened. "Blaine—"

"But I need to stay. I don't want to break up, but I have to stay."

I pushed my thumb and middle finger into my eyes until it hurt. "Then we won't break up."

"We have to."

"Long distance," I said, shifting. "I can do long distance."

I heard her crying.

"Like I said, I have a lot of PTO." I swallowed, trying to open up my throat. "And I'm pretty good at texting."

Another full minute passed. Just breathing and sniffling came through her end of the line. My knuckles started to hurt—I hadn't realized I'd been holding the phone so tightly.

Please, Blaine, I wished, hoped, prayed. *Please work with me.*

Finally, after what felt like an eternity, she whispered, "I love you."

I straightened, the weights in my organs lifting some. My pulse reverberated in my ear and bounced against my phone. In the silence of the stairwell, I said, "I think I love you too."

After we hung up, I bought another plane ticket for Palouse for that weekend. I wouldn't be able to do more until Infrared cleared up.

But Blaine was worth the wait.

Chapter 17

MOM GOT WORSE. A lot worse.

But then she started getting better.

I kept her on a good, heart-healthy diet, and fortunately I had an amazing boyfriend back in Utah who knew a thing or two about nutrition, so whenever I had a question or needed help with meal planning, he was on the other end of the phone or sending me GIFs of dancing vegetables. By February, her risk of a heart attack dropped substantially, and by March, her dialysis trips dropped from three to two per week.

I missed Lysander a ton. I missed Rue too, who helped me pack up my things after Thanksgiving, when Tess was able to fly out for a week so I could box up my life in Utah. But seeing my mom every day, even under less-than-ideal circumstances, was really nice. We'd always been close. There was a sense of comfort in our new normal.

I loved the Palouse too. Maybe not winter in the Palouse—I preferred Utah's salt-everything technique to Eastern Washington's let's-just-scatter-small-rocks-everywhere one, but you could see a lot more stars in the sky at night, the weather was milder, and there was no smoggy inversion. In March and April, little sprigs of green wheat started dotting the rolling farm hills, and by summer they were long enough that, when the wind blew, it felt like I was standing in a waving emerald ocean.

Our farmers markets were way better too.

And I liked my job, which was a relief. The people I worked with were kind and *way* more liberal than my Utah colleagues. My supervisor was sane. No one microwaved fish TV dinners in the break room. And I had a knack for marketing, apparently.

I never did get to see little Patrick, Nora's baby. But she sent me lots of photos of him and kept me apprised of the latest IO Masters technical writer drama. Carol was, miraculously, canned, and all the world rejoiced. Nora was promoted, and three more technical writers were hired on, including the contractor who got stuck with my Infrared leftovers.

Derby went on as derby does. Spokane had a small team, but Spokane was an hour and a half away, so while I'd gotten acquainted with the members, I didn't make any official practices or games. But that was okay. Some things had to be sacrificed for better things.

Mom and I went on daily walks once winter thawed, which was part of her doctor-approved exercise regimen. Lysander joined us on weekends once or twice a month, when he could get away. He'd meant it when he said he could make long distance work. I was still too concerned to leave my mom's side long enough for a trip to Utah unless someone

was staying with her, so 90 percent of the traveling fell to
Lysander. I tried to make it up to him by sending him care
packages and risqué text messages.

> **Me:** Got this new bra. What do you think? Too
> lacy?

> **Lysander:** Definitely not too lacy . . .

By the end of summer, Mom was doing well. Really well,
actually. Well enough that I didn't worry about her when I
was at work or if I wanted to take a longer trip into Spokane
or Lewiston. It crossed my mind, on occasion, to look for job
in Utah again, but I *did* like working for the University of
Idaho, and I enjoyed sharing a house with my mom. Plus . . .
if something else happened to her, I didn't think I'd forgive
myself.

This was a topic of conversation that came up often during
my and Lysander's nightly phone calls. Minus Fridays, which
were gaming nights. Man needed his role-playing outlet.

October popped up before I knew it. I'd missed Halloween last year, so I was excited to make the most of the holiday
season this time around. The town put on a festival called
Haunted Palouse, which was one of my all-time favorite
things. I used to volunteer to be one of the grotesque displays
along the path of the hayrides, but this year I just wanted to
enjoy it. Tonight, three days before Halloween, Mom was
going with me to browse the vendors; in our shared bathroom, I brushed and curled my hair. I'd swapped out the
electric blue for purple in August. Didn't dress up in costume,

but did put on a corset over my blouse, because why the heck not?

"Are you ready?" I called out as I thumbed through my makeup basket for my plum lipstick.

"Oh, in a bit."

I rolled my eyes and applied the color to my pout. My mom permed her short hair and didn't believe in makeup, so getting ready for her was, like, a sneeze. You blinked, and she was done. But she was definitely dragging her feet today.

I paused my administrations and swept out of the bathroom to where she sat at the kitchen table, ready to go save for her unshod feet. "Are you feeling okay?" I asked, stepping closer to give her a good once-over. "You can't fake it till you make it anymore, Mom."

Now she rolled her eyes. "I'm fine. Just checking my email."

I snorted. "Nobody emails you."

She shrugged. "Some people do."

I turned for the bathroom. Hesitated. "Are you on a dating site?"

Glancing up at me, she waggled her eyebrows. "Ooh, there's an idea."

Sighing dramatically, I ventured down the hallway to her bedroom, crouching down at her closet floor to get her a pair of shoes. She had a pair of loafers that would look cute and were good for walking in, but I wasn't sure how warm they'd be. "Do you want loafers or boots?" I called. I heard her shuffle around in the kitchen—and if I could hear that, she could definitely hear me. "Loafers or boots, Mom?"

After a beat, she said, "Boots, please!"

I grabbed a pair of navy ankle boots and headed up the hall. "All the good stuff's going to be gone by the time we get there—"

The last word died in my mouth as I entered the kitchen. My mom was gone, tucked away somewhere, and Lysander stood in front of the sink, a sheepish smile on his beautiful mouth, his hair newly cut, beard newly trimmed, and he was wearing a *dress shirt* and it wasn't even Easter.

"Ly!" I dropped the shoes and ran to him, hugging him hard enough to push him back into the sink. I only noticed he was holding flowers when the cellophane crinkled against my hip. Pulling back, I cupped his face. "You said next week, right? I wasn't expecting you!"

"Surprise," he said, and kissed me, and I sensed my mother in my periphery but I did not care. I kissed Lysander with everything in me—I always did, because our kisses and embraces were so far apart, and I never knew when I'd get my next chance. It was the suckiest part about a long-distance relationship.

I pulled away and grinned at him as he rubbed my back, then turned to the flowers. "Peonies! How did you get peonies this time of year?" I took the bouquet from his hand. "I assume they're for me?"

"Unless I've been dating your evil twin," he remarked.

Beaming, I scooted over to a high cupboard where we kept the vases, standing on my tiptoes to reach the closest one. Lysander appeared behind me and grabbed it for me.

"Thanks!" I paused at the sink and checked my watch. "No, you were planning to come next week. Am I crazy?"

He shrugged. "I figured I'd come up early and check out my new digs."

I turned on the faucet. Filled the vase. Paused. "Wait, what?"

He smiled, a sort of lazy half smile that made gooseflesh prickle my arms. "I got a job. At Washington State University. I start a week from Monday."

I shrieked and tipped the vase over, sending water up and over the rim of the sink. "You got a job? Here?" I pressed wet fingers into my unset makeup. "You're moving here?"

His smile only widened. "I'm moving here."

I screamed before tackling him and pressing plum-colored kissed all over his lips and jaw. "You butthead! You didn't even tell me you were looking!"

He grabbed my waist and laughed. "I didn't want to get your hopes up. It's *hard* to get a job around here."

I swatted him. "Yeah, I know!" Hugged him again. "Ly, this is amazing!" I paused, glancing back to my mom, who was being oddly catlike, hanging out in the corner like that. "But what about your family?"

His hands rose from my hips to my shoulders, then glided down my arms to my hands. "You took a break from yours. I figured I can do the same."

My vision misted. I squeezed his hands. "That is the most amazing thing you've ever—"

Lysander dropped down to one knee.

"E-Ever . . ." I trailed as he reached into his pocket. As all my air left me, I managed to ask, "Wh-What are you doing?"

Hot and cold engulfed me as he pulled out a cardinal ring box and opened it, revealing a gold band with a circle-cut diamond nestled against a crescent peridot—my birthstone. "Blaine Stephanie Wickers."

The mist turned into tears which turned into gushing Niagara waterfalls down my face. *Now* I understood why my mom had dawdled, and why she watched so quietly from the corner. Now I understood why Lysander had come early. Why he had brought flowers.

Now I understood why all of it, even the YouTube video, was worth it.

"Will you marry me?" he asked, and didn't stutter once.

And, of course, I said yes.

THE END

Acknowledgments

FIRST, THANK YOU to everyone who made it to the end of this book. This is a new adventure for me, and I appreciate it!

Second, a huge thank-you to my husband, who makes it possible to write with two littles running around. I'd always toyed with the idea breaking from fantasy to do a contemporary romance, but didn't have enough of a spark to do it . . . until I went on a date with said husband to Slapfish and told him about the idea for this novel. We talked about it, and suddenly I really wanted to make it happen. So, Jordan, thanks for the spark!

I would be remiss if I did not give a wild amount of thanks to my life manager (aka editor) Kristy S. Gilbert, who not only helped me with editing and formatting this book, but actually seriously kind of runs the background of my writing life. Newsletters, websites, graphics . . . I would lose my head without her. (That's why the book is dedicated to her. She deserves it.)

Thank you so much to Caitlyn McFarland, my bestie and partner in podcast, who had to explain to me on the phone how contemporary romance novels work after reading my initial outline for this and who helped me fix the roughest spots of the story. LOVE YOU.

Thanks to Emily Schwarzmann, who besides being a walking billboard for everything I write, acted as my go-to for all my roller derby questions.

And to my brother-in-law Chad Loiseau, who helped me figure out how IT management and motorcycles work.

Huge thank-yous to Leah O'Neill, Whitney Hanks, and Rachel Maltby, who yet again got me feedback on the story in very quick time and who were willing to jump genres with me as well. I owe you guys a lot. And huge thank-yous to last-minute feedback from Kanisha Chandler, Mimi KL, Deborah Deitcher, Lisa Cook, Melissa Baker, Hallie Dell, Sarah Drummond, Jenn Cooper, Brekke Felt, Amy Lauderback and Stephanie Augustine.

My appreciation to the Queens of the Quill—my indie support group who took me under wing and explained how self-publishing works. I had a lot of dumb questions for them. I *still* have a lot of dumb questions for them. They win the patience award.

And, as always, a big thank-you to my Heavenly Father, who is also mucho patient with me and is the giver of All The Things. <3

If you enjoyed this novel by C. N. Homberg, check out some of her award-winning and best-selling fantasy novels (with kissing in them). She publishes her fantasy work under the name Charlie N. Holmberg.

TTHE PAPER MAGICIAN SERIES
The Paper Magician
The Glass Magician
The Master Magician
The Plastic Magician

THE NUMINA SERIES
Smoke & Summons
Myths & Mortals
Siege & Sacrifice

THE SPELLBREAKER SERIES
Spellbreaker
Spellmaker

THE STAR MOTHER SERIES
Star Mother
Star Father

STANDALONE NOVELS
Followed by Frost
Magic Bitter, Magic Sweet
The Fifth Doll
Veins of Gold
The Will and the Wilds

CPSIA information can be obtained
at www.ICGtesting.com
Printed in the USA
JSHW051931240222
23274JS00004B/13